District

Wreaths, Arrangements & Basket Decorations

Wreaths, Arrangements & Basket Decorations

Using Flowers, Foliage, Herbs and Grasses to Make Colorful Crafts

Ellen Spector Platt

Rodale Press, Emmaus, Pennsylvania

The author and editors at Rodale Press hope you will join with us in preserving nature's beauty so that others may share in the enjoyment of nature crafting. Unless you are certain that the plants or plant materials you are collecting—including leaves, stems, bark, flowers, fruits, seeds, or roots—are very common in your area, or over a wide geographic area, please do not collect them. And do not disturb or collect any plants or plant materials from parks, natural areas, or private lands without the permission of the owner.

To the best of our knowledge, the plants and plant materials recommended in this book are common natural materials that can be grown and collected without harm to the environment.

Executive Editor: Margaret Lydic Balitas
Senior Editor: Cheryl Winters Tetreau
Copy Manager: Dolores Plikaitis
Copy Editor: Laura Stevens
Office Manager: Karen Earl-Braymer
Administrative Assistant: Susan Nickol
Editorial Assistance: Deborah Weisel
Art Director: Michael Mandarano
Book Designers: Patricia Field and Darlene Schneck
Cover Designer: Linda Jacopetti
Photographer: Mitch Mandel
Illustrator: Frank Fretz
Indexer: Nanette Bendyna
Photo Stylist: Ellen Spector Platt
Assistant Stylist: Toni Groff

Special thanks to the following for lending props:
 Laura Brubaker, Kutztown, Pa. (quilts)
 Maria DiCesare, Orwigsburg, Pa. (spools and threads)
 Mona Gavigan of Affrica, a gallery in Washington, D.C. (Kente cloth)
 Judy Hummel of The Monogram Shop, Orwigsburg, Pa. (spools and threads)
 Leesport Antiques, Leesport, Pa. (glass bowl)
 Toy Barn, Orwigsburg, Pa. (toys)

If you have any questions or comments concerning this book, please write to:

Rodale Press, Inc.
Book Readers' Service
33 East Minor Street
Emmaus, PA 18098

Library of Congress Cataloging-in-Publication Data

Platt, Ellen Spector.
    Wreaths, arrangements & basket decorations : using flowers, foliage, herbs and grasses to make colorful crafts / by Ellen Spector Platt.
        p.   cm.
    Includes bibliographical references (p.   ) and index.
    ISBN 0–87596–587–3 hardcover
    1. Dried flower arrangement. 2. Flower arrangement.
3. Wreaths. 4. Baskets. 5. Nature craft. I. Title.
SB449. 3. D7P59 1994
745.92—dc20   93–42957
                                                              CIP

Distributed in the book trade by St. Martin's Press

2 4 6 8 10 9 7 5 3 1 hardcover

OUR MISSION

We publish books that empower people's lives.

RODALE 🌱 BOOKS

For Benjamin B. Platt,
the visionary

■

Contents

Acknowledgments

*I*n putting this book together, I enlisted the aid of almost everyone I know. No one was safe. I mention these people to whom I am particularly grateful.

Toni Groff and Emily West Platt lent their creative design ideas as well as beautiful objects and assisted with the photo styling. Thanks to Max and Toni Groff for allowing us to photograph in their beautiful home. Chad Goehring, Sebastien Sohier, and Valerie Loger all toiled in the garden the summer we were growing the huge variety of flowers used in the book. Barb Pressler and Sharon Linard graciously allowed me to pluck their blooms when I needed just the right color. Treesa Lipkin encouraged me to prowl in her home and borrow whatever I needed. Dolores Delin and Evelyn Diamond also lent their treasures. Mary Ann Conway, quilter, spinner, and dyer, offered many excellent suggestions on dyeing with natural materials. Leila Kern, Esq., once again resolved all of my contract issues with her customary grace. Ben Platt, M.D., book salesman extraordinaire, helped me with my computer needs, as well as with fresh bread for the film crew.

To all authors everywhere, I wish as harmonious and delightful an experience as I have had working with the editorial and artistic staff of Rodale Press. My particular thanks go to Cheryl Winters Tetreau for editing with humor and making sure I wrote with clarity; to photographer Mitch Mandel for his artistic eye and the technical skills to match; to illustrator Frank Fretz, who has an intimate understanding of the flowers I grow; to Trish Field, for her original book design; and to designer Linda Jacopetti, whose unseen hand is behind each photograph. I also want to thank Troy Schneider and Nancy Ondra for their special contributions. I want to give particular thanks to Maggie Balitas, executive editor, who provides the leadership for a collection of people to function as a team and to get it right.

Introduction

*W*hen Dorothy awoke in Oz, her world ricocheted from stormy black and white into a Technicolor fairyland. The surprise created on the big screen was stunning; the colorful impression has remained with me since childhood.

This book helps you create color-filled surprises with flowers. It shows you the effects you can produce by a quick immersion into color.

Interior designers have long acknowledged that changing the color of accessories is the least expensive, most dramatic way of enhancing a room. Try this experiment. Examine a room layout in your favorite home magazine. Mentally remove the vase of scarlet tulips on the sideboard, the bowl of lemons on the coffee table, or the violets crammed into a silver basket on the bedside table. In your mind's eye, remove all fresh or dried produce and arrangements. Immediately the room reverts to a duller, less interesting version. As you page through the magazine, you'll notice that the life of a room is often concentrated in the colors of the flowers and fruits that decorate it.

Rainbow-hued flowers, herbs, foliage, fruits, and vegetables are readily accessible for your own color experiments. Whether you grow your own, buy from a florist and dry your own, or go to the market for your materials, you can find what you need for special effects if you select by color.

I grew up in a home with one sister, two parents, and three sets of childless aunts and uncles. The women agreed on what colors were proper for the home; brown, gold, and green were basic. For excitement, they introduced rust or henna. Blue was considered avant-garde. There could be no deviation from the family color dictates.

Nice girls wore pastels, soft creams, whites, and beiges. Navy blue was mandated for the spring wardrobe. Browns were acceptable; purple was not. Black was for funerals—and nightclubs, which were for "others," not us.

But we often had flowers from the garden stuffed informally into one of our four vases: daffodils in the clear glass, marigolds in the pewter, crimson roses in the white pottery, and, every fall, a new crop of bittersweet in the brown pitcher.

With marriage, my exotic and rebellious color choices encompassed white walls, white china, and blond wood. Later, with small children and little money, chocolate brown and cocoa seemed practical choices, with burnt orange added for accent.

As my experience and budget expanded, I enlarged my palette, but childhood habits die hard and I kept reverting to the old favorites.

When I started Meadow Lark Flower & Herb Farm, I planted predominantly yellow flowers, indulging my taste for their sunny look. I stuffed the cutting beds with 'King Alfred' daffodils, 'President Kennedy' tulips, showy yellow dahlias and zinnias, golden gloriosa daisies, several shades of huge yellow marigolds, and, for drying, 20 feet of yarrow and globe centaurea. Since I eschewed pinks and purples in decoration, I avoided these colors in the garden as well.

Then I tried to sell my flowers. Local florists were impressed with the freshness, quality, and variety, but one dealer explained that customers want flowers to match the interior of their homes; the predominant colors then were blue, peach, and mauve. She told me brides choose anything but yellow.

The cheerful dried tansy, yarrow, and centaurea remained in my barn, while my small stock of pink and blue larkspur, wine-striped love-in-a-mist, and blue globe thistle flew out the door. First lesson learned: Pay attention to color.

Second lesson: Dried flowers fade in the natural order of things. Bright sunlight and humidity hasten the fading. I wanted to sell dried flowers that would be as brilliant and as true as possible. I learned the best ways of drying, what varieties and colors to plant, how to care for arrangements after they were made to keep the colors from fading, and when to toss the whole thing on the compost pile. Despite what I read in copy from overly imaginative advertising writers, nothing lasts forever, including dried flowers.

Given that fresh flowers will last for one to two weeks in my home, I became daring without saddling myself with expensive, permanent mistakes. Experiments with flower color were easy and achieved dramatic results. I urged customers who were trying to match their wallpaper or fabric to include a contrasting color so the whole arrangement wouldn't fade into the background. We tried pink and red with peach, dabs of yellow with blues and lavenders. I was encouraged by the enthusiastic responses.

I started choosing containers for color as much as for style and expanded my personal and retail collection of interesting containers. I noticed how a green container for dried flowers increased the fresh look of the arrangement. I tried rejuvenating unattractive containers with a color application.

A strange thing happened on my way through preparing this book. I was ostensibly writing about designing *flowers* with color, but color considerations permeated my other decisions. When my dining room needed repainting, I chose blue and yellow—a completely novel combination for me. With my dining set badly marred and desperately needing rejuvenation, I chose a colorful paint design instead of refinishing the rosewood veneer. When my peach living room needed a fresh application of paint, I went two shades more intense than the previous pastel.

Even my wardrobe mysteriously evolved. With my dark hair and fair skin, true red was a favorite. Suddenly I started gravitating to fuchsia reds and cobalt blues—not quite electric blue, but shocking for me. My favorite new silk scarf mixes purple, orange, navy, fuchsia, and gold into galactic swirls of color.

It is my fervent hope that you will not just try some of the designs in this book but that you will also adapt them to your own color needs—and above all—have fun experimenting with color and creating your own surprises.

ELLEN SPECTOR PLATT

CHAPTER 1

COMBINING THE COLORS

...

Understanding Color Concepts

My fourth-grade teacher tacked a large color wheel to the bulletin board and tried her best to instill in us some ideas about primary, secondary, and complementary colors. She expected the class to paint balanced designs obeying these color principles. The paint boxes she distributed were a rare treat, doled out on those few occasions when the fat, awkward crayons wouldn't serve; in this case, the lesson was on mixing colors.

I always opened my paint box with suspense. These same boxes were shared by the entire school, passing from one class to another. If the previous user hadn't bothered to rinse her brush after each use, I knew the little tins would all be a muddy brown on the surface. If my predecessors had heavily favored one color, that tin would be half gone and full of hairs shed by the cheap little brushes. But if, as I hoped, several colors were almost used up, then a supplication to the teacher would result in brand-new paint tins to replace the empty ones. Oh, the fascination of dropping water from the brush onto the pristine surface and watching the true, unsullied color emerge! The actual lesson about the color wheel paled in importance beside the opportunity of puddling around in the clear, rich colors.

Although I never learned to draw or paint, my fascination with color remains. I take great pleasure in experimenting with color in my flower design and craft work and watching how adding or subtracting a color can change the whole feel of the design. Sometimes it's merely a question of finding a wonderful background color to highlight an arrangement, or changing the light source to illuminate a project. Other times I must add or subtract a contrasting color to change the design from ordinary to exciting, or from raucous to calming. While you might not want to change your basic home colors very often, you can change the color of crafts that enhance your home space and not just match what you already have. The same basic ideas of the color wheel still apply, but now they seem more understandable and certainly more useful than they did in fourth grade.

The Color Wheel

The rain just stopped on a warm summer's eve. Over Hawk Mountain to the east, the wide arc of a rainbow shimmers, filling the sky. Someone calls out. Everyone rushes into the meadow to catch the ephemeral sight. We know what to expect and are not disappointed. The colors are always the same and in the same order. The rainbow glows, fades, and is gone.

If we pass a beam of pure white sunlight through a glass crystal known as a prism, the light breaks up into the same rainbow of hues. It is the color spectrum, ranging from red through yellow, green, and blue to violet. The colors are always in the order of the rainbow. When these colors are arranged in a circular fashion, we refer to the format as the color wheel, which shows the relationships of one color to another. Although principles of mixing light colors and paint colors are slightly different, these differences don't need to concern us here. If, as you design your crafts, you keep referring to the color wheel, you'll get some new insight and help with your color questions.

On the color wheel are three primary colors: red, yellow, and blue. They are called primary because all other colors are a combination of amounts of these three. No combination of other colors can produce any one of these three.

The secondary colors are mixtures of equal amounts of two of the primaries. Mix red and yellow and you get the secondary color orange; mix yellow and blue and you get the secondary

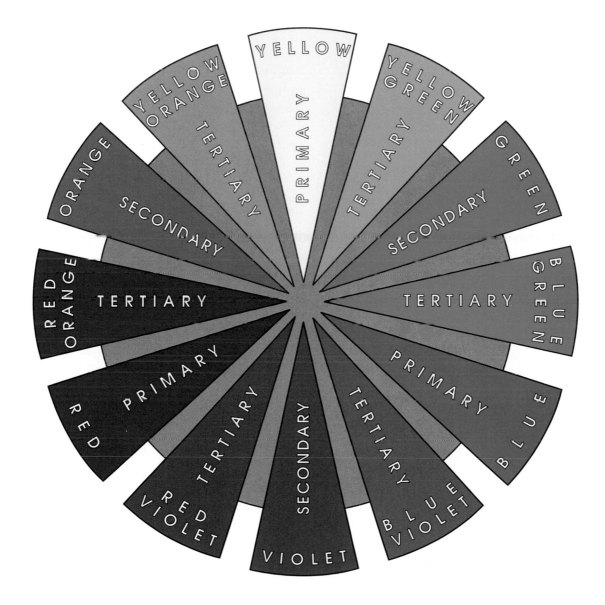

color green; mix blue and red and you get the secondary color violet. If you stopped here you would have a 6-color wheel. But you can expand the color wheel to 12 colors by mixing a primary color and one of its secondaries to give a tertiary (third) color; mixing yellow and green gives yellow-green; mixing yellow and orange gives yellow-orange. These clean, pure colors

True reds, yellows, and blues always look fresh and vibrant in combination. On the first day of summer, an assortment of yellow snapdragons, yarrow, 'Moonbeam' coreopsis, blue delphiniums, scarlet sage, and Maltese cross (*Lychnis chalcedonica*) issue a primary-color wake-up call.

■

are referred to as hues. I will use the terms color and hue interchangeably to refer to the quality of blueness or redness or greenness of an object. By giving colors romantic names like "wild cornflower," "Georgia peach," and "cinnamon rose," manufacturers hope to induce us to buy their paints, fabrics, and carpets. But those names also cause confusion. Is "Confederate blue" bluer or grayer than "Williamsburg blue"? How does "Aspenwood" compare with "briny deep"? The names of the color wheel are more mundane, but they help us avoid confusion. By referring to the color wheel, we can derive many pleasing color schemes that might not readily come to mind when designing a craft. Have you ever tried an arrangement based on the primary colors?

Complementary Colors

The colors directly opposite each other on the color wheel are called complementary colors; thus, yellow and violet are complementaries, as are green and red, and orange and blue. We often use complementary pairs in traditional holiday decorations: yellow and violet for Easter, red and green for Christmas. But these pairs used full strength may seem too surprising or harsh for year-round use in home furnishings. When either black or white is mixed into the colorant, complementaries become more similar to each other and, to many people, more pleasing. Mixing white paint into red and green gives two pastels that are often used together for a romantic look. Think of pink rosebuds on ivory wallpaper with pale green leaves and stems.

Sometimes a complementary color is just what we need to add some zip to a craft project just because of the intense contrast. Remember that in adding a complementary color, you needn't add equal amounts in volume—a little of the complement goes a long way toward adding interest without being garish.

Adjacent Colors

Look at the color wheel again. You can't go wrong in designing a project if you choose an adjacent (analogous or neighboring) color scheme—that is, using two or more colors lying right next to each other on the color wheel. Of course, not every hue is represented by just these 12. If we had paint pigments, we could continue mixing adjacent colors to achieve hundreds of new subtle combinations. Use your imagination to fill in all of the hues between green and blue-green—all of the aquas, for example. But if you select any 3 colors that are next to each other, like yellow, yellow-green, and green; or red-violet, red, and red-orange, I think you will be very pleased with the results. If you are not accustomed to working with hot, intense colors, this adjacent color scheme will give you a never-fail guide.

If the main color you want to use is not on the wheel, use your imagination to conjure up the hues that would be next in the spectrum in either direction. I started with the fuchsia hat in the photo on page 6 and went to purple-red, red-orange, and orange-yellow for my accents. (See page 52 for project instructions.)

Intensity

The colors on the wheel are bright, intense, and clear. They represent the full force of the hue. If you were mixing paints and wanted to tone down the intensity of a color, you could add a small amount of a complementary color to make it duller. As you add a larger and larger proportion of the complementary, the two colors will cancel each other out, forming a gray, or muddy, neutral color. For example, if you want to tone down a very bright red paint, you can add some green to

The purple and blue flowers are a vibrant contrast to the subtle variations of yellow, gold, and orange in this rhododendron print.

■

dull the red. If you add too much, you will neutralize the red completely until you have a rather unappealing gray. When you are designing crafts with flowers and other plant materials, the colors are already there for you. Nature did the color mixing; you must make the selection. However, if you want to either paint a container or add a needed touch of color, understanding the basic concept of intensity will enable you to avoid many unhappy mistakes.

Tone

Adding white to a hue changes the tone, making it lighter—a pastel. We speak of

Venture into unusual color territory with a fuchsia hat basket decorated in adjacent colors like red and orange.

■

"tints" of a color when it is mixed with white. Pink is a tint of red, made by adding some white. Tints are young, happy, spring-like. Adding black to a hue also changes the tone, making it darker. We call this a "shade." Maroon is a shade of red. Shades can be somber, antique-looking. Recent trends in Christmas colors use shades of red and green rather than the pure hues that were popular for so many years. The combinations of wine red and forest green are more muted and now more pleasing to many people. Perhaps in another generation the pastel tints will be in fashion; pink and pale green will be the colors in vogue for Christmas.

Harmony of Intensity

Extremes are often jarring, out-of-whack, unnerving. With harmony, we think of balance, calm, satisfaction. But we don't want to be bored and put to sleep by dullness. If all of the hues are the same intensity, there will be a harmony. Think of the neon colors, like neon red, neon lime, and neon yellow, which look better with each other than with other colors because the intensities are in harmony, although all are jolting. Make a color scheme in which each of your colors harmonize by using them in the same intensity. In the mitten wreath on page 14, the blue-green, purple, and red-purple are about the same intensity and thus are harmonious. (Instructions for making the mitten wreath begin on page 46.)

Harmony of Tone

The pastels are tints of the hues in the color wheel. With equal amounts of white added to these colors, they all fall into a harmonious relationship. Any of the pastels look good together if they have the same proportion of white in their makeup. Also, any of the shades look good together with a commonality of black in their makeup.

Harmony of the Complement

Harmony of the complement is achieved in a three-color scheme. Take any key color for your main selection. Look across the color wheel for the complement, then find the two colors on either side of the complement. These two are called the split complement of your key color. If yellow is your key color, then blue-violet and red-violet are the split complements. With plant materials, you will often wind up with the split complements when you try to match because flowers come in hues that are difficult to match exactly. So much the better—see the project on page 108, where I tried to get complementary fresh flowers and wound up with a color range.

The Neutrals

White, black, and gray are not part of the color spectrum, but they are important neutrals, both in color mixing and in highlighting other hues. In flower arranging and in garden design, the addition of gray foliage cools down hot colors and unifies most other garden schemes. Plants with gray foliage such as artemisia, lamb's-ear (stachys), or verbascum (mullein) have a unifying effect when distributed throughout a multicolored garden. This foliage has the

This sitting room is decorated primarily with neutrals. The overall effect is serene and cozy. The dried flower swag on the old locust basket maintains neutrality but adds interesting texture and form to the design.

■

same unifying effect when a flower design needs an added "something" and you're not sure what. White often stands by itself or with gray in the design of an evening moon garden. I sometimes add one variety of white flowers to an otherwise monochromatic design to relieve the monotony. With dried-flower projects, the whites are particularly important because the natural light reflectance of dried flowers is much lower than that of fresh flowers. The arrangements often need some white to lighten and highlight the other colors. I plant plenty of white cleome, zinnias, lilacs, roses, phlox, mums, scabiosa, and snapdragons to add to fresh arrangements; and baby's-breath, statice, strawflowers, larkspur, and pearly everlasting to use fresh or dried.

The color green stars in much of our natural surroundings. It is one of the secondary colors, and you can choose to treat it as an important color selection and feature it in a craft project. When working with fresh or dried flowers, however, the meaning of the color green often changes. Since we are accustomed to thinking of foliage as background for the more interesting and fragrant blooms, green becomes a neutral in most flower arrangements. We often aren't aware that it's there; it becomes a background color. When I talk about color schemes, I will generally ignore the bits of green that show on stems and foliage, unless it is an important feature of the design.

I resist the temptation to add masses of green leaf fillers to every arrangement as florists sometimes do as a way of enlarging without greatly increasing the cost. It's better to have fewer flowers in a smaller container where each bloom can be shown to best advantage. Save the greens for places where you truly want them in the design for themselves.

Color and Light

We perceive colors as if they are part of an object. We say the book is green, the lemon is yellow, but, in fact, color is a property of light. Different surfaces have the ability to absorb and reflect different parts of the color spectrum. So a lemon absorbs all of the colors of the light spectrum except yellow. This yellow light is reflected back to our eye, and we perceive it as the color of the lemon. When there is no light, the same lemon looks black.

It is obvious to anyone who ever painted or decorated a room, or tried to select paint swatches or match fabrics, that colors appear different during daylight than they do in the evening hours when incandescent lights are on in most homes. In fact, colors look different in the different seasons as the position of the sun changes in the sky, and indoor colors change almost by the hour as the sun moves through the heavens and shifts the light coming in our windows. Indoors, fluorescent light usually makes things look bluer, including skin tones.

Surface texture also affects how much light is reflected from an object back to your eye. Certain petals (or bracts) that are shiny when dried, like those of strawflowers, reflect more light than duller ones, like those of dried larkspur; thus, strawflowers appear lighter.

When selecting colors for a craft design, check them first (when possible) under the kind of light conditions that you have in your home. If you put a dark wreath in a dark hallway, you know that there will be very little color reflectance. Think of either adding a light source to the hallway or making sure you use light colors and lots of white in your wreath.

Although bright sunlight can gradually fade dried flowers, indoor lighting isn't as harmful. I try to place my best dried-flower arrangements near a good lamp or under a ceiling spotlight to take advantage of the added reflectance. Sometimes all it takes to make a difference between a dull and exciting arrangement is increasing the wattage of the bulb (if the fixture can accept it). As a temporary measure for a special event, you can position your craft on a bright windowsill. Don't leave it there permanently if you care about prolonging the intensity of the colors.

Here is an example of a dried arrangement with an additional light source. The colors of fresh flowers are not as affected by the absence of a good light source. The moisture in the petals increases the surface reflectance, making the colors appear vivid even under low-light conditions.

This arrangement has a light source trained on the flowers. They spring to life when the lamp is switched on. With the lamp off, the edges of the room are dim and the dried flowers fade into the scene.

■

A monochromatic wreath of yellow-green feels quiet and restful against a honey-colored wall.

■

Place the same wreath against a persimmon background and the flower colors pop.

■

Background

You've probably noticed that you get more compliments when you wear certain colors. That's because your skin reflects the fabric colors near your face. For example, those with sallow skin should avoid wearing yellow and beige tones near the face because they increase the yellow quality of the skin almost to the point of making it appear jaundiced. In the same way, flowers reflect the colors of their surroundings. When you position a craft object or arrangement, the background color becomes part of the whole. Factors like contrast, reflectance, and texture become important. Look at the series of photos on this page to see how the mood of one object changes with a different background color and the accent of a complementary color. By moving your craft to a new site in your home, you can change the whole feeling of the project.

Add orange accents to match the background and purple for intense contrast. Now the original yellow-green serves mainly as a foundation for the other colors.

■

CHAPTER 2

DESIGNING
WITH
COLOR

■ ■ ■

Choosing a Color Scheme

Where do you start when deciding on a color scheme? Many of the most satisfying color schemes come from fantasy, stimulated by the colors of nature. Picture the ever-changing colors of the moon. Rather than let some preordained combination dictate your arrangement, call upon lunar visions of opal, silver, palest yellow, and gleaming ivory. Make an arrangement using only these colors. Or think of the colors of the sun. They change with time of day, time of year, and other less pleasing variables like smog conditions. Let the colors of a glorious sunset that lives in your memory stimulate a craft in brilliant yellows and the shades of gold, crimson, and wine.

Of course, you don't have to take all of your inspiration from nature—look around your own home for ideas on color schemes. Take a color inventory of your furniture and drapery fabrics, favorite art, china patterns . . . the list goes on. Making wreaths and arrangements fit into your decor is effortless when you keep a particular furnishing in mind as you craft.

Holidays are other inspirational events that call to mind some very traditional colors. Use these as a jumping-off point for your own holiday crafts.

Whether you choose color schemes from nature, decor, or remembrances of holidays past, your personal color preferences shouldn't be overlooked. You probably have favorite colors that give you a feeling of comfort and security; perhaps you also have colors that you loathe. Colors have the power to create certain moods. Some of these moods are learned by associating a color with certain key experiences and are thus idiosyncratic. For example, I hated the awful long, pink snuggies my mother made me wear as a child to keep warm in winter, and for years would select nothing pink to wear or have around me. If the hospital room you stayed in after your tonsillectomy was a dull shade of green, you may never choose that color for your home.

Part of the reaction to color may be unlearned or at least learned in the same way by most other people. We speak of warm and cool colors. The hues of reds, oranges, and yellows and their mixtures are the warm colors of sun and fire; the hues of greens, blues, and violets are the cool hues of water, grass, and forests. If you have a north-facing room or a part of the house where the heater is most inefficient, decorating or accenting with warmer colors actually makes most people feel less cold. Conversely, in the summer or in warmer climates, cool color accents provide a bit of soothing relief from oppressive heat and humidity.

The concepts of the color wheel provide a comfort when you are trying to devise an unusual color scheme for a project. You can experiment freely with color in flower design without either breaking the bank or being stuck with a permanent mistake. Go ahead, be daring!

Color Schemes Based on the Color Wheel

Expand your palette by referring to the color wheel on page 3. There you will find combinations that may not leap readily to mind. By choosing a color scheme based on the wheel—using colors that are primary, complementary, adjacent, or monochromatic—you can risk trying a combination you have never tried before and the result will not be disappointing.

Primary Scheme

This color scheme involves using mainly pure red, pure yellow, and pure blue. These don't have to be in equal proportions; some people think a little red goes a long way. Feature the blue or yellow if you wish and add touches of the other two primary colors. Add some white or gray as desired.

Complementary Scheme

This is a two-color scheme. Refer to the color wheel on page 3 and pick one important color. Choose accents in the complementary color—the color directly opposite on the wheel. For example, if blue is your main color, use small amounts of orange for an unusual color accent.

Split-Complementary Scheme

This is a three-color scheme. Again, refer to the color wheel on page 3 and pick one important color. Then find its complement directly opposite it on the wheel. But instead of using the complement, choose the two colors on either side of the complement; these are the split complements. So if blue is your main color, orange is the complement, so you'll choose the two colors on either side of orange to go with the blue. The result:

You will have a scheme of blue, yellow-orange and red-orange.

Adjacent Scheme

This is one of the easiest and, to my eye, the most satisfying of all schemes, whether in the garden or in the home. You merely select two, three, four, or even five colors (as I've done for my hat basket on page 52) lying right next to each other on the color wheel. Start anywhere on the wheel and add the neighboring colors from either side. You can derive very hot schemes if you start with red-violet and go clockwise on the color wheel to red, red-orange, and orange. You can derive very cool schemes in the same way. Start with red-violet and select the hues in the counterclockwise direction: violet, blue-violet, blue, and blue-green.

Monochromatic Scheme

This scheme uses one hue and as many variations in tone and intensity as you can find. The color match won't be perfect when

A monochromatic color scheme of oranges imparts a fall feeling on this old barn door.

■

you are using natural materials, but the project will be all the more interesting.

Although a few green leaves and stems sneak in, the fresh floral decoration shown on page 13 is all tones of orange. When deciding what hue to use as your central theme, consider the variety of materials available on that day. On a fall day, orange predominates in my garden, so the decision about this wreath was easy.

For an outstanding fresh arrangement, try using only white flowers, perhaps with some gray foliage for contrast. Use bleached pods like milkweed or unicorn plant (*Martynia* spp.) as accents.

A summer arrangement of all greens—with flowers like green nicotine plant, "Green Envy" zinnias, and bells-of-Ireland mixed with variegated foliage like hosta's—looks cool and refreshing on a hot day.

Somewhere there is a mitten heaven where all lost mittens congregate. On this wreath, they have sorted themselves into a harmonious unit.

Experiments in Harmony

Harmony in art, like harmony in music, consists of combinations that are pleasing rather than discordant. Harmony describes agreement among the various elements. In flower design, you can create harmony by simplicity; use more stems of a few flowers rather than one stem of lots of different kinds of flowers. The repetition of elements creates harmony. You can achieve harmony in color by using monochromatic or adjacent color schemes, or by working with tone or intensity.

Harmony of Tone

Try a pastel color scheme using materials of the same tint, that is, all with the same strength of white added to the hue. Use two to six different pastels, taking pale versions of the six primary and secondary colors. Choose from pale yellow, pale orange, pale pink, pale green, pale blue, and pale violet, as I've done for the covered basket shown on page 96.

Harmony of Intensity

Another way of achieving color harmony is to work with each hue at the same level of intensity. In the mitten wreath on the left, the vividness of each individual color is balanced by the vividness of all of the others, leading to a pleasing combination.

The Colors of Nature

Start with one of the abundant combinations provided by nature as filtered through your memory and whimsy. Recall the colors of an evening sky, a deep forest, an arid desert, a country meadow, a luxuriant pond; think of the hues of earth and rock or the brilliant colors of jewels.

Picture the Caribbean Sea from a low-flying airplane. The crystal-clear water seems arranged in undulating color bands by some unseen artist. Where the water is deep, the sea looks navy blue. In the next band, the sunlight is reflected through brilliant aqua water. Where the gentle waves lap the shore, a pale aqua tint looks most inviting.

Aqua is not one of the popular interior colors in the northeastern United States, perhaps because here we seldom see these colors as part of nature. However, along the Florida coast where the ocean, inlets, and canals are part of daily life and in the Southwest where lodes of turquoise are still mined, various hues of green-blue and blue-green are ever in fashion. When I want to work with a fresh color scheme, I conjure up the varying colors of the sea for inspiration. (See page 80 for my still-life interpretation.)

The Colors of Home

If you don't use the inspiration of nature, then you may consider borrowing from human inspiration. Your fabric, wallpaper, paintings, china, and vases have each been designed by a person who tried to create something beautiful, unusual, and colorful.

In starting a craft project, perhaps you will begin by thinking of a painting that has been hanging above a mantle over the years. Do you walk by and scarcely notice it anymore? Examine it carefully. Pinpoint the dominant color, the various tints and shades, the color accents and contrasts. Select a color for your arrangement that highlights one of the color accents or one of the background colors of the painting. Use that as your major theme.

Instead of a painting, you may choose to start with a wallpaper design, a favorite vase, or the pattern of your china. Take inspiration from the colors that you see. You may want to choose for your wreath, arrangement, or basket decoration a color theme that is secondary to the design of the china or wallpaper rather than in the dominant color.

The Colors of the Holidays

Think of yellow and purple decorations for Christmas; green and red for Easter. This makes us uneasy; something feels wrong. We have traditional colors for most of our holidays, and most of us want them to stay that way. The tones may change with fad and fancy, but not too much. While bright green and bright red may be traditional Christmas colors, the shades of wine red and forest green have recently become very popular. The glimmer of metallic decorations enhances other tones. Ice blue and silver have their place at Christmastime. But too much peach or pink and we look askance.

Patriotic holidays in most countries flaunt the colors of the flag; red, white, and blue for the Fourth of July and blue, white, and red for Bastille Day in France make us remember past glories. Decorations for the African American celebration of Kwanzaa often reflect the black, red, and green of the African National Congress flag, the flag of the anti-apartheid movement.

For Valentine's Day, candy shops occasionally display yellow satin hearts with yellow lace, blue hearts with violet flowers, or other traitorous combinations. But only tones of red—from crimson to palest pink—look truly authentic for Valentine's Day.

An American Thanksgiving celebration borrows its colors from those of the harvest: orange pumpkins, golden corn, the pale wheat color of grains and grasses, and the crimson of cranberries and apples.

Color is the main reason that flower crafts seem appropriate for the holidays. I will show some ways of adding to the richness of your holidays by building on the color themes.

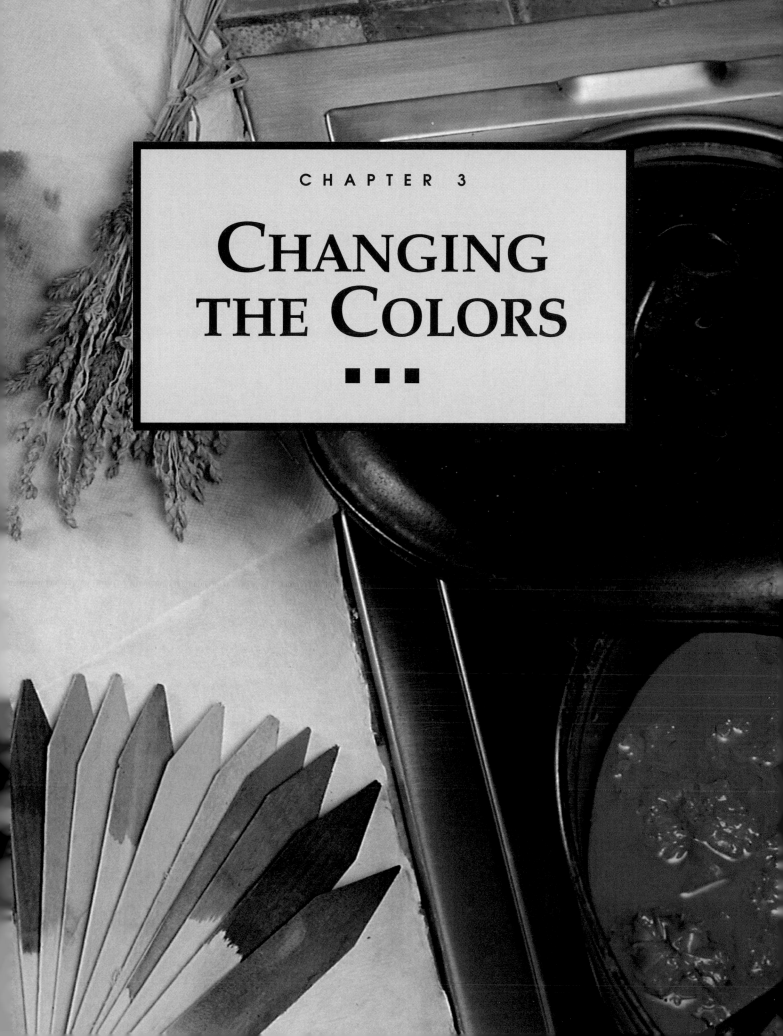

CHAPTER 3

CHANGING THE COLORS

■ ■ ■

Using Natural Color Variations

*P*aint stores are bursting with luscious colors to brush, spray, stencil, sponge, dip, or spatter on baskets, wreaths, and even dried flowers themselves. Any hue imaginable can be matched exactly using the precise formulas at your local dealer. Baskets come painted, stained, and dyed in all sorts of magnificent colors, and I am often attracted to a basket because of its color.

In this chapter, I want to show you how you can change the colors of plant materials, wreaths, baskets, and other containers—but by using only natural methods. You won't have the full range of hues to work with—the colors will be more subdued than the intense artificial ones—but the challenge is in changing the colors in natural ways, and the satisfaction will be in the discovery process.

Color Control

Start having control over the colors of dried plant material by selecting and planting (or buying) the cultivars that best retain their colors when dried. Flowers always lose intensity of hue when they dry. In general, you must begin with a vivid, fresh color in order to have a pleasing dried color.

Reds

In addition to roses, the true reds are best represented by the many cultivars of cockscomb, both the plumed and crested culti-

vars. The fire-engine, slightly orangey reds dry to a popular tone for Christmas. Those cultivars that have some purple in their fresh stage dry to a rich burgundy velvet. Other good reds are 'Strawberry Fields' globe amaranth, smooth sumac, scarlet sage, rose hips, pepperberries, and dried pomegranates.

Oranges

Orange is the best keeper in dried flowers. Try to work some in where you need a vivid color. In addition to globe amaranths and strawflowers, try heliopsis, Japanese lanterns, gloriosa daisies, and sunflowers.

Yellows

Yarrow and tansy are staples of the flower drier's garden. Goldenrods, marigolds, annual yellow statice, and, of course, the yellows of strawflowers are other important contributors. Try *Helipterum sanfordii* for small, vivid globes of gold.

Greens

Very few plants remain green when dried. Bells-of-Ireland will disappoint every time as you watch the intense green fade to a parchment beige in six months. Undyed eucalyptus turns a gray-green when dried, a pleasant color that has its place but really is more gray than green. For a better green, dry boxwood, salal, bear grass, galax, bay laurel, Scotch broom, rose leaves, or oriental nigella.

Blues

In most garden catalogs, purple and lavender flowers are called "blue." If you are particular about your colors and have a plan in mind for a true blue garden, selections are sparse. Among the perennials are bearded iris, veronica, and delphinium. Among the annuals are bachelor's-button, morning glory, and love-in-a-mist. For dried flowers, the selection is even more limited. My favorites are 'Ritro' globe thistle, 'Blue Boy' bachelor's-button, 'Nikko Blue' hydrangea, and those few larkspurs in a pack of mixed seed that can break away from their purple parentage. The wildflower viper's bugloss (*Echium vulgare*) is a lovely shade of true blue when dried, but it is very prickly to work with.

Violets

Many cultivars of purple flowers abound. My favorites are fragrant lavender, larkspur and the related perennial delphinium, ageratum, various shades of purple and lavender-blue statice, sage ('Victoria' or 'Superba'), and pressed pansies.

Whites

For a flower that is true white when dried, look to strawflower, winged everlasting, pearly everlasting, and other white everlastings like German statice. White larkspur and feverfew become creamy in color, and white roses look like antique ivory. Make up your mind that what you need is not a brilliant pure white but a slightly mellow hue.

The Color of Roses

Deep-red roses. Those luscious long-stemmed American beauties that are often chosen as gifts to a beloved always dry a dark, blacklike shade. If you want a *red* dried rose, start with an orangey cultivar like 'Mercedes'

or 'Tropicana'. Palest pink roses will fade too much in the drying process. If you want a dried pink rose, start with a coral pink like 'Queen Elizabeth', or the climber 'America', or a vivid pink-purple like 'Prive'.

The Color of Wood

Usually when we think of the color of a wreath we think of the decoration—the flowers, leaves, bows, and other adornments. Using the photo below as a guide, try experimenting with different color twigs and branches when you make your next wreath,

Make small wreaths from nontraditional branches for unusual color effects. Here, clockwise from the top, are wreaths made from catbrier, yellow-twig dogwood, fantail pussy willow, willow, bittersweet, and multiflora rose; the center wreath is made from red-twig dogwood. These materials were all cut in winter.

■

and work with color from the base up. Once you start looking at the colors of branches and vines, you'll find that even the browns take on very different hues. Birch has a definite red tinge, while grapevine is a dull gray-brown. For added interest, make small wreaths out of red-twig dogwood when the color is at its most vibrant in late winter. Cut some branches of yellow-twig dogwood if you are looking for a yellow-toned wreath. Catbrier (*Smilax spp.*) is bright green in winter and will maintain that color for many months if hung on an outside door. It becomes more brown as it dries but still retains a green, khakilike tinge. For a plant that stays dark green even when dried, use Scotch broom. You will have a lovely forest green to highlight any color decoration. Of course, pussy willow wood with its silvery buds always looks interesting. Search for other woods and notice their color changes throughout the year. Pick the branches to enhance your decorating scheme.

Color Change in Sweet and Sour Soil

Certain cultivars of hydrangea are notorious for changing color when the soil is either too acidic (they turn more blue) or too basic (they turn more pink). Many of the newer cultivars have been bred for stability of color despite soil conditions, but if you have one of the older varieties and you want to vary the color of the hydrangea blossoms, add some lime for more pink or, for more blue,

Harvesting for Color Variation

An intriguing way to control the color of flowers or plant materials is by picking at different stages of maturity. After drying, flowers are particularly affected by the stage at which they were picked. For example, rosebuds dry a deeper color than the flowers. Here's when to pick for the best dried color.

PLANT MATERIAL	PICK EARLY FOR:	PICK LATER FOR:	PICK LATEST FOR:
Dock	Green	Peach	Chocolate
Goldenrod	Green	Gold	—
Hydrangea, 'Nikko Blue'	—	Blue-violet	Blue-green
Japanese lantern (pod)	Green	—	Orange
Peegee hydrangea	—	Pink/green	Wine
Safflower	Green	Orange	—
Sensitive fern (pod)	Green	—	Brown
Teasel (pod)	Green	—	Gray-brown

add some acidic fertilizer (the kind meant for azaleas); follow package directions for mixing and applying.

Dyeing with Plant Dyes

You can make your own dyes and stains using plant materials that you grow or buy at the market. Using beets, dahlias, red cabbage, purple basil, nuts, and other vegetation, you can achieve wonderful muted hues with which to dye dried flowers and grasses or to color baskets and containers. Children will be entranced with making and using their own dyes. In addition to dyeing flowers and baskets, use your dyes to tint Easter eggs and absorbent paper for gift wrap.

Dyeing with natural materials is a grand experiment rather than an exact science. No matter what recipes you follow for making dyes, the color of your dye bath can vary greatly depending on many factors including these:

- The type of soil your plants were collected from. Naturally occurring chemicals in the soil can change the hues of the dye.
- The hardness or softness of the water in which you simmer the plant material. Hard water has a high iron content and iron tends to make dyes darker.
- The nature of the chemical additives to the water, such as fluoride and chlorine.
- How long and at what temperature you cook the plant material.
- The nature of the material to be dyed. Wool and other animal hair like angora dye a much more intense color than plant materials like flowers, reeds, and cotton.
- What kind of pot you cook the dye in. Stainless steel, enamel (chipless), and Pyrex glass are nonreactive, but cast iron, copper, and aluminum can affect the colors of the dyes.

- How the finished project is displayed and stored. Natural dyes are not colorfast in light and will fade somewhat over time.

How to Make Dyes

Many of the dyes shown in the photo on page 22 are made solely by simmering plant material and water until the plant releases its color substance. Pick 2 or more cups of plant material, rinse quickly to remove dirt and bugs, put it in a pot, add water to just cover, and simmer until the desired color is released. (This can take anywhere from 30 minutes to 3 hours.) Then strain and add flowers, eggs, or baskets to be dyed. If desired, paint the dye on a basket with a brush.

To get a more intense color, you can add a mordant while the mixture simmers. Mordants are additives that help keep dyes colorfast and increase the intensity of the hue, sometimes changing it completely. When you are dyeing wool or cotton materials that will be washed or dry-cleaned over the years, a mordant plays a much more important role than it does in dyeing flowers, grasses, and baskets.

Here, I have only used two harmless mordants: alum straight from the spice department in the supermarket and iron released from the cast iron cooking kettle. Use about 1½ tablespoons of alum per batch of dye. Other less benign mordants commonly used by dyers are copper sulfate, chrome, and tin.

How to Use Natural Dyes

As I mentioned earlier, there are no absolutes when it comes to dyeing with natural dyes—you should be prepared for a few unpleasant color surprises when you begin. However, that doesn't mean you can't have some control over the process. Whether you're dyeing flowers or other plant material, baskets, containers, or eggs, you want to be sure to get good results, even if the colors aren't always what you expect. Here are some tips that will help you achieve that goal:

- Try to enhance a natural color rather than change colors completely. Don't try to make a pink flower yellow or a green leaf pink. Instead, dip leaves in green dye to augment natural color, dip faded flowers in dye to revive their color.
- Start with a dried flower with a good, firm structure, not one that is broken or falling apart.
- Light-colored flowers and grasses usually take a dye best, for example, faded flowers like bells-of-Ireland, and wheat or anything you have that's light beige.

Make natural dyes from plant material to tint flowers, grasses, and baskets.

■

- Some plant material has a natural waxy coat that causes any dye to "bead up" and not stick. If that happens in your test batch, add three drops of liquid dish detergent to the dye. It will change the surface tension and allow the dye to adhere.
- When choosing containers or baskets for dyeing, look for ones made of raw wood or wicker and that haven't been painted, dyed, or shellacked. To dye a basket, you can dip it in the dye bath or paint on several coats of dye with a small brush.
- To dye eggs either for Easter or to use as vases (see page 142), add three drops of liquid dish detergent to the dye or bath. Or dip the shell in water to which 6 drops of vinegar have been added and then dip it in the dye. Either method will breach the waxy coat of the egg, allowing the dye to adhere.
- Before dyeing a whole bunch of flowers, test one flower in the dye bath to make sure you are pleased with the result; if you don't like it, you'll only have wasted one flower.
- To deepen the color on a flower or basket, allow the material to soak in the dye bath for several hours, or paint the object with two or three coats of dye, letting each coat dry before adding another.
- Use plenty of newspaper or other coverups to prevent spills on countertops, or dye in a garage or outdoors.

Fading and Bleaching Flowers, Pods, and Grasses

Sun will fade the colors of dried flowers. Normally, my advice is to keep dried flowers away from windowsills or bright sunlight because they will fade drastically within six months. There are times, however, when you want a faded color, perhaps a softer tint of an intense orange, magenta, or crimson. Or perhaps you want the soft beige, ivory, and parchment tints that come with aging green grasses and grains. In those cases, find your sunniest spot and have some patience. From a bright orange globe amaranth you will get a nice peach color; from magenta you will have pale pink. I sun-fade flowers for one to two months so they will lose the vivid coloration that I strive for in most of my design work.

If you want a brighter white, perhaps for a Christmas or winter project, try bleaching pods. Follow these simple steps:

1. Use one-third liquid bleach to two-thirds water.

2. Soak pods like teasel, martynia, okra, and others in the liquid for one to two days.

3. You may have to weight down your plant material, as it has a tendency to float in the bleach solution. Use clean, non-porous weights such as jars filled with water and capped.

4. Remove the plant material from the solution, rinse, and spread it out in the sun for a few hours, turning it over once.

Changing the Color of Containers

A dramatic way to improve old, cracked, uninteresting, or unattractive containers is by "tiling" them with petals and leaves. The coffeepot pictured on the right had lost its lid many years ago and was useless as part of a formal china set. I made the "matching" lid from a demitasse cup that had lost its handle and was ready for the recycling can. Use bottles or glass of any shape for a translucent effect when the project is complete.

Glue fresh plant material directly to the clean container. The material dries in place, leaving unusual patterns on the container. Use a toothpick or other small stick to apply white craft glue directly around the edges of each petal or leaf. Start applying the glued "tiles" to the mouth of the container. Continue gluing on the leaves or petals in rows. Overlap each piece at least ¼ inch. The tiles will shrink when dry and allow some of the old container to show if the material isn't overlapped well.

The best leaves for tiling are soft and pliable when fresh, so they will conform easily to the shape of the container. My favorite is lamb's-ear because it stays soft and velvety even when dry (as in the photo below). Other good leaves to use are galax (on the two round bowls), flowering plum (on the bottle), and rose. Petals of gloriosa daisy stay bright and colorful when dried on the container. Experiment with other leaves and petals to see which you prefer.

To improve the appearance of old china and glass containers, "tile" them with petals and leaves.

■

CHAPTER 4

KEEPING THE
COLORS

■ ■ ■

Maintaining the Color in Your Crafts

*I*f you plant the best cultivars and harvest the flowers at the best stage, or if you've bought the freshest flowers imaginable, you still have important work to do in order to save the colors. You must follow conditioning, watering, and drying guidelines in order to get the best possible color from both fresh and dried flowers.

Conditioning Fresh Flowers

If you've ever gone to a flower show the day after it opens and have seen a magnificent arrangement with a few flower heads drooping, you know that the flowers were not properly conditioned. If you are given a bouquet of roses and after only three days in the vase, half of the heads hang down as if they are nodding in shame, you probably have a conditioning problem. Conditioning refers to proper care of fresh flowers before you start to arrange them.

If you are working with flowers from your own garden, pick them in the early morning or early evening to stop them from drooping in the hot summer sun. In cool spring weather, the time of day for picking isn't so critical. Get the cut flowers in water as soon as possible. Many books recommend taking a bucket of water out to the garden for this purpose. I think lugging a heavy bucket around the garden, sloshing as you go, is an unnecessary fanaticism, provided you are fairly faithful about the other details.

Once the flowers are in your house, strip off the bottom leaves. Fill tall containers with warm water and add flower preservative according to package directions. Recut the stems on an angle with a very sharp knife or clippers. Plunge the flowers immediately into the containers. Do not submerge leaves; if you do, they will start to decay. Decay shortens flower life. Anyone who has ever discarded a vase of old, improperly treated flowers can recognize the slime and stench of bacterial decay.

Don't crowd your container. Flowers that are crowded together can begin to mold. Leave the containers of flowers in a cool, dim place for several hours or overnight before you begin your arrangement. Condition foliage and herbs for your crafts the same way.

These procedures help to prolong the life and color of the flowers and foliage once you arrange them. If you are using floral foam rather than plain water, conditioning is even more important because it is harder for most flowers to drink from foam than from water in a vase.

Certain flowers have additional requirements for conditioning. Florist's roses and gerber daisies are often wired up their stems and through their heads as a mechanical way to prevent drooping. Here are three tips for the trickiest of plant materials:

1. Flowers that wilt easily: For roses, gerber daisies, hollyhocks, gloriosa daisies, and other troublesome flowers, fill your sink with 5 inches of water. Cut at least 1 inch off their stems under water before putting them in the conditioning containers. You may notice bubbles exuding from the stems as you cut. The bubbles are air that has lodged in the stem; if it isn't released, this air will block the uptake of water in the containers, causing "the droops."

Using the same method, you can often revive gift roses that are in a foam base and starting to droop after several days. Remove them from the arrangement, recut their stems under water, plunge them in a container of warm water, and let stand for several hours. They will often perk back up with this treatment, and you can safely replace them in the arrangement.

2. Plants with milky sap: For poppies, poinsettias, dandelions, euphorbia, and other stems that contain a milky sap, recut the stem under water, then sear the bottom with a candle or gas flame, or rub it briefly on a hot burner unit of your electric range. This little bit of extra care prevents these flowers from "bleeding" to death.

3. Woody shrubs: For lilacs, viburnums, and other finicky woody shrubs, smash the bottoms of the stems with a hammer or make a number of vertical cuts for 3 inches up the bottom of the stems and plunge them in very warm, deep water to condition. Remove all leaves that are not essential to your arrangement. Sometimes I strip all of the leaves off a lilac stem to help direct all of the water to the flower rather than to the thirsty leaves; then, I pick other stems of lilac foliage to mix in with the flowers. Even with all this work, lilacs are still chancy to condition. Forsythia, though woody, needs no special care.

Aftercare

You must continue to add water to flowers every day or so after they are arranged. Even

Buying Fresh Flowers

Shoppers stand in the produce section of the supermarket carefully selecting the blackest, firmest bing cherry in the bin; they heft and smell the cantaloupes to try to divine the sweetness within; they eschew the pale green-beans with rust spots as they cull the basket for young ones. Flowers, whether in the supermarket or at your florist, give off similar clues to freshness.

To get the freshest materials, learn when new deliveries are made. Many florists get a fresh flower delivery every day, but some of these may languish in the cooler for a week or more before you enter the shop. And before that, at the wholesaler's, some flowers don't "move" quickly and hang around getting crushed until they are put on special. Locally grown flowers are usually (but not always) fresher than flowers that come from abroad. Learn which were just delivered. The condition of foliage gives an excellent clue. If the bottom of the flower stem is brown and old looking, the flower has already been in water for a long time. Flower stems can be cut, but the lower foliage will give another clue: It should be firm and free of slime and translucency.

Keep in mind, however, that if you restrict your purchases to those flowers that have the longest natural vase life, you will miss some of the glories of the flower world. Look for flowers not fully unfurled so they can mature in your home. If you have a problem with your flowers, most florists want to know about it so they can correct it, and they will often replace the flowers if, for example, they never open at all. But remember that it's up to you to condition your flowers properly to ensure that they look their best.

if there is flower preservative in the water, heavy drinkers may drink the vase dry before their natural vase life is over. I visited the Museum of Modern Art in New York and couldn't help but notice that a magnificent 4-foot arrangement of fresh flowers in a glass vase at the information booth was drooping badly, although the flowers didn't seem to be old. The water level had been allowed to drop to 4 inches from the bottom, and many of the shorter stems were completely out of water. Did I bring it to their attention? You bet I did, although I think I was judged a busybody.

Flowers in foam especially need extra water. One reason (other than the heat) that flowers in hospital rooms die after only two days is because few people think to water them and they completely dehydrate.

Keep fresh flowers as cool as possible—not over a radiator or on a sunny windowsill—to prolong their life and color. Direct drafts are just as harmful as direct heat. A fan or air conditioner blowing on flowers will quickly dry out the delicate tissues.

Some Die Early

Different flowers have different life spans in a vase no matter how careful you are about proper care. Blossoms of the German iris or gladiolus will bloom for only several days, although another bud will open in that time. To keep your arrangement fresh looking, groom the flowers and foliage every two days. Snip off fading blossoms to rejuvenate the whole arrangement.

If many of the flowers are over the hill but a few stalwart chrysanthemums, carnations, or lisianthus remain healthy, save those few stems before chucking the lot. Wash and recut the rescued flowers and rearrange them in a much smaller container, perhaps with new foliage or bare twigs from your garden. I par-

ticularly appreciate this new arrangement because I have rescued the flowers from a too early demise on the compost heap.

Drying Fresh Flowers

Certain flowers that keep their form well when dried look good only in certain colors. In general, white flowers (other than true everlastings like strawflowers and globe amaranths) fade to beige after drying, so if you want to dry marigolds, choose yellow or orange, not any of the new whites. Deep red roses like 'Mr. Lincoln' will turn a purple-black when dried, so for a vivid red, dry 'Tropicana' or 'Mercedes'. Yellow cockscomb dries a very soft honey beige; for a vibrant color, select one of the bright salmon, pink, or red shades.

For best quality, start the drying process

Keeping the Color in Dried Flowers

After you have learned the specifics of flower drying described in Chapters 1–4, refer to these six simple rules to get the most color from your dried flowers:

1. Know which flowers dry well (not all do).

2. Start with high-quality flowers with the best color.

3. Pick at the proper stage of development.

4. Select a suitable method for drying.

5. Dry as quickly as possible, where it is warm, dark, and not humid.

6. Once dried, display away from direct sunlight and in as dry an atmosphere as possible.

with a healthy, sound flower, not one whose petals have already started to brown. Of course, you will also want to dry and keep flowers that have sentimental value—just don't expect them to reverse the dying process and suddenly have good color after they are dried.

Here at Meadow Lark Flower and Herb Farm, where we dry wedding bouquets, prom corsages, and other special flowers, we accept them only one or two days after the event, even if they have been well taken care of—otherwise, the results are very disappointing.

Flowers that are already over the hill and have opened too far may disintegrate further after drying. If you've ever picked and dried mature Scotch thistle or Joe-Pye weed, you have probably chased fluff around the room trying to clean up shattered seeds. These flowers need to be picked in their bud stage for drying, even though they are less dramatic in that form.

Drying Methods

There are several methods for drying flowers and foliage. It's important to match the method to the plant materials you are working with. I use these methods: air drying, oven dehydration, pressing, desiccant drying, and microwave drying. Here's a look at each technique.

Air Drying

This method allows warm, dry air to circulate around the flowers. Wrap a bunch of five to ten stems with a rubber band and hang them in a warm, dark, dry spot. (Use opened paper clips to make little hangers, as shown in the illustration above.) Let them hang for one to two weeks until the flowers are dry. The length of time it takes to dry the flowers will depend on the humidity in the air, the amount of water in the flowers, and the number of flowers you are drying.

Air-dry flowers with flat flower heads, like Queen Anne's lace or gloriosa daisies, on an old window screen, as shown below. Poke holes through the screen. Insert the stems in the holes, so the flower heads rest on the screen. That way they will dry flat and opened. I also use screens for drying flower heads that I will be using for gluing, where no stem is required. Scatter the flowers in a single layer on the screen and allow them to dry in the warm air.

(continued on page 38)

Best Plants for Drying

Plant	Easy to Start from Seed or Cutting	Growing Requirements	Color When Dried	Best Drying Method
African daisy (*Lonas annua*); annual	S	SU	Gold flowers	Air
Ageratum, 'Blue Horizon' (*Ageratum houstonianum* 'Blue Horizon'); annual	S, I	SU	Lavender flowers	Air
Alliums (*Allium* spp.); perennial bulb	—	SU	Lavender or white flowers; beige seed head	Air
Amaranth, 'Green Thumb' (*Amaranthus caudatus* 'Green Thumb'); annual	S	SU	Green flowers	Air
American bittersweet (*Celastrus scandens*); shrub	—	SU	Gold seedpods; orange berries	Air
Annual statice (*Limonium sinuatum*); annual	—	SU	White, rose, salmon, purple, or yellow flower heads	Air
Apple mint (*Mentha rotundifolia*); perennial	C	SU	Purple flowers	Air; press
Apple-of-Peru (*Nicandra physalodes*); annual	S	SU	Green to brown seedpods	Air
Artemisia, 'Silver King' (*Artemisia ludoviciana* 'Silver King'); perennial	—	SU	Gray foliage	Air; press
Astilbes (*Astilbe* spp.); perennial	—	SH, M	Pink flowers	Air
Baby's-breath, 'Perfecta' (*Gypsophila paniculata* 'Perfecta'); perennial	S	SU	White flowers	Air
Bachelor's-button, 'Blue Boy' (*Centaurea cyanus* 'Blue Boy'); annual	S	SU	Blue flowers	Air; silica
Balloon vine (*Cardiospermum halicacabum*); annual	S, I	SU	Green seedpods	Air
Barley (*Hordeum vulgare*); annual	S	SU	Green or beige seed heads	Air

KEY		
S = start from seed	I = best started indoors	SH = part shade
C = start from cutting	SU = needs full sun	M = extra moisture

PLANT	EASY TO START FROM SEED OR CUTTING	GROWING REQUIREMENTS	COLOR WHEN DRIED	BEST DRYING METHOD
Bee balm, 'Cambridge Scarlet' (*Monarda didyma* 'Cambridge Scarlet'); perennial	S, C, I	SU	Deep pink flowers	Air
Bells-of-Ireland (*Moluccella laevis*); annual	S	SU	Green flower spikes	Air
Blackberry lily (*Belamcanda chinensis*); perennial	—	SU	Dark purple seeds	Air
Bougainvillea (*Bougainvillea* spp.); vine	—	SU	Fuchsia bracts	Air
Boxwoods (*Buxus* spp.); shrub	C	SU	Green foliage	Air
Bright star (*Helipterum humboldtianum*); annual	—	SU	Bright gold flowers	Air
Brooms (*Cytisus* spp.); shrub	—	SU	Green stems	Air
Buttercups (*Ranunculus* spp.); herb	—	SU	Yellow flowers	Air
Butterfly weed (*Asclepias tuberosa*); perennial	S, I	SU	Orange or yellow flowers; brown seedpods	Air
Catmint (*Nepeta* spp.); herb	S, I	SU	Lavender flowers	Air
Chinese lantern (*Physalis alkekengi*); perennial	S, I	SU	Green or orange pods	Air
Cinnamon fern (*Osmunda cinnamomea*); perennial	—	M	Dark brown spore stalk	Air
Cockscomb, 'Floradale' (*Celosia cristata* 'Floradale' series); annual	S	SU	Pink, red, or yellow flowers	Air
Common hops (*Humulus lupulus*); perennial	—	SU	Green "cones"	Air
Common tansy (*Tanacetum vulgare*); perennial	C	SU	Gold flowers	Air
Common toadflax (*Linaria vulgaris*); perennial	—	SU	Yellow flowers	Air; press

(continued)

KEY		
S = start from seed	I = best started indoors	SH = part shade
C = start from cutting	SU = needs full sun	M = extra moisture

Best Plants for Drying—Continued

Plant	Easy to Start from Seed or Cutting	Growing Requirements	Color When Dried	Best Drying Method
Contorted hazel (*Corylus avellana* 'Contorta'); shrub	—	SU	Brown stems; greenish yellow catkins	Air
Cooking sage (*Salvia officinalis*); perennial	—	SU	Gray leaves	Air
Coral bells (*Heuchera sanguinea*); perennial	—	SU	Pink or rose flowers	Air; press; silica
Craspedia (*Craspedia globosa*); perennial	—	SU	Gold flowers	Air
Crookneck loosestrife (*Lysimachia clethroides*); annual or perennial	—	SU	White flowers	Air
Delphinium, 'Pacific Giant' (*Delphinium × elatum* 'Pacific Giant' series); perennial	S, I	SU	Purple-blue flowers	Air; press; silica
Dogwoods (*Cornus* spp.); tree	—	SU	Pink or white bracts	Silica
Edelweiss (*Leontopodium alpinum*); perennial	—	SU	White flowers	Air
Fountain grass (*Pennisetum setaceum*); annual or perennial	—	SU	Pink seed heads	Air
Foxtails (*Setaria* spp.); annual or perennial	—	SU	Green seed heads	Air
Fragrant cudweed (*Gnaphalium obtusifolium*); annual or perennial	—	SU	White flowers	Air
German statice (*Limonium* spp.); perennial	—	SU	White flowers	Air
Globe amaranth (*Gomphrena globosa*); annual	S	SU	White, pink, or purple flowers	Air
Globe centaurea (*Centaurea macrocephala*); perennial	S, I	SU	Gold flowers	Air

Key		
S = start from seed	I = best started indoors	SH = part shade
C = start from cutting	SU = needs full sun	M = extra moisture

PLANT	EASY TO START FROM SEED OR CUTTING	GROWING REQUIREMENTS	COLOR WHEN DRIED	BEST DRYING METHOD
Globe thistle (*Echinops ritro*); perennial	S, I	SU	Blue-gray flower heads	Air
Gloriosa daisy, 'Double Gold' (*Rudbeckia hirta* 'Double Gold'); perennial	S, I	SU	Gold flowers with brown centers	Air (on screen)
Gold-and-silver chrysanthemum (*Chrysanthemum pacificum*); perennial	—	SU	Yellow flowers	Air
Goldenrods (*Solidago* spp.); perennial	—	SU	Gold flowers; green leaves	Air; press
Green lavender cotton (*Santolina virens*); perennial	—	SU	Green foliage; cream flowers	Air
Hare's-tail grass (*Lagurus ovatus*); annual	S	SU	Beige seed heads	Air
Heather, 'H. E. Beale' (*Calluna vulgaris* 'H. E. Beale'); shrub	—	SU	Pink flowers	Air; press
Helipterum (*Helipterum roseum*); annual	S	SU	Pink or white flowers	Air
Honesty (*Lunaria annua*); biennial	S	SU	Pearly white inside green seedpods	Air
Horsetail (*Equisetum* spp.); perennial	—	M	Green stem	Air
Hydrangea, 'Nikko Blue' (*Hydrangea macrophylla* 'Nikko Blue'); shrub	—	SU	True blue flowers	Air; press
Immortelle (*Xeranthemum annuum*); annual	S	SU	White, pink, or lavender flowers	Air
Japanese fantail willow (*Salix sachalinensis* 'Sekka'); tree	C	SU	Brown stems	Air
Joe-Pye weed (*Eupatorium purpureum*); perennial	—	M	Mauve flowers	Air
Lady's-mantle (*Alchemilla mollis*); perennial	—	SH, M	Yellow-green flowers	Air

(continued)

KEY		
S = start from seed	I = best started indoors	SH = part shade
C = start from cutting	SU = needs full sun	M = extra moisture

Best Plants for Drying—Continued

Plant	Easy to Start from Seed or Cutting	Growing Requirements	Color When Dried	Best Drying Method
Lamb's-ear (*Stachys byzantina*); perennial	C	SU	Gray leaves	Air
Lavender (*Lavandula angustifolia*); perennial	S, I	SU	Lavender flowers; silvery leaves	Air
Lemonleaf salal (*Gaultheria shallon*); tender shrub	—	SU	Green leaf	Air
Lion's ear (*Leonotis leonurus*); annual	S, I	SU	Orange flowers	Air
Love-in-a-mist (*Nigella damascena*); annual	S	SU	Green-and-brown striped seedpods	Air
Love-lies-bleeding (*Amaranthus caudatus*); annual	S	SU	Wine-colored flowers	Air
Masterwort (*Astrantia major*); perennial	—	SU, M	Silver flower heads	Air
Monkshoods (*Aconitum* spp.); perennial	—	SH, M	Purple flowers	Air; press
Mountain mint (*Pycnanthemum tenuifolium*); perennial	C	SU	Green leaves	Air
Mulleins (*Verbascum* spp.); biennial	S	SU	Brown seed stalks	Air
Multiflora rose (*Rosa multiflora*); shrub	—	SU	Coral to red fruit	Air
Orange globe amaranth (*Gomphrena haageana*); annual	S	SU	Orange or red flowers	Air
Oregano (*Origanum vulgare*); perennial	—	SU	Purple flowers, green buds	Air
Oriental fennel flower (*Nigella orientalis*); annual	—	SU	Green seedpods	Air
Pampas grass (*Cordateria selloana*); annual or perennial	—	SU	Pink flowers	Air
Pansy (*Viola × wittrockiana*); annual	—	SU	White, yellow, rose, orange, or purple-blue flowers	Silica; press

---

KEY

S = start from seed   I = best started indoors   SH = part shade
C = start from cutting   SU = needs full sun   M = extra moisture

PLANT	EASY TO START FROM SEED OR CUTTING	GROWING REQUIREMENTS	COLOR WHEN DRIED	BEST DRYING METHOD
Pearly everlasting (*Anaphalis margaritacea*); perennial	—	SU, M	White flowers	Air
Peegee hydrangea (*Hydrangea paniculata* 'Grandiflora'); shrub	—	SU	Greenish to pink flowers	Air; press
Pennyroyal (*Mentha pulegium*); perennial	S	SU	Lavender flowers	Air
Pentzias (*Pentzia* spp.); annual	S	SU	Gold flowers	Air
Peonies (*Paeonia* spp.); perennial	—	SU	Pink or red flowers	Air; oven; silica
Peppergrass (*Lepidium virginicum*); annual	—	SU	Greenish brown seedpods	Air
Periwinkle (*Vinca minor*); perennial	—	SH, M	Green foliage	Air; press
Plumed celosia, 'Century' (*Celosia cristata* 'Century'); annual	S	SU	Yellow, cream, red, or pink flowers	Air
Poinsettia (*Euphorbia* spp.); houseplant or tender perennial	—	SU	Pink, red, or coral bracts	Silica
Poppies (*Papaver* spp.); annual	S	SU	Gray seedpods	Air
Purple coneflower (*Echinacea purpurea*); perennial	S, I	SU	Mauve flowers	Air (on screen)
Purple loosestrife (*Lythrum salicaria*); perennial	—	M	Magenta flowers	Air
Pussy willow (*Salix caprea*); shrub	C	SU	Silvery buds	Air
Quaking grass (*Briza maxima*); annual grass	S	SU	Beige seed heads	Air
Queen Anne's lace (*Daucus carota* var. *carota*); annual or biennial	—	SU	White flowers	Air (on screen); press

(continued)

KEY		
S = start from seed	I = best started indoors	SH = part shade
C = start from cutting	SU = needs full sun	M = extra moisture

Best Plants for Drying—Continued

Plant	Easy to Start from Seed or Cutting	Growing Requirements	Color When Dried	Best Drying Method
Rat-tail statice (*Psylliostachys suworowii*); annual	—	SU	Mauve flowers	Air
Roses (*Rosa* spp.); shrub	—	SU	Red, pink, or white flowers; reddish fruit	Air; oven; press; silica
Safflower (*Carthamus tinctorius*); annual	S	SU	Green buds; orange flowers	Air
Sage, 'Blue Bedder' (*Salvia farinacea* 'Blue Bedder'); annual or perennial	S, I	SU	Blue flowers	Air; press
Scarlet sage, 'Early Bonfire' (*Salvia splendens* 'Early Bonfire'); annual	S	SU	Red flowers	Air; press
Sea hollies (*Eryngium* spp.); perennial	S, I	SU	Blue-gray flower heads	Air
Sedum, 'Autumn Joy' (*Sedum* × 'Autumn Joy'); perennial	C	SU	Mauve to chocolate-brown flowers	Air
Sensitive fern (*Onoclea sensibilis*); perennial	—	M	Chocolate brown spore stalk	Air
Sheep sorrel (*Rumex acetosella*); perennial	—	SU	Green to pink or brown seed heads	Air
Siberian dogwood (*Cornus alba* 'Sibirica'); shrub	—	SU	Red stems	Air
Smooth sumac (*Rhus glabra*); shrub	—	SU	Red seed heads	Air
Sneezeweed, 'The Pearl' (*Achillea ptarmica* 'The Pearl'); perennial	—	SU	White flowers	Air
Sorghum (*Sorghum bicolor*); annual	S	SU	Brown-and-cream seed heads	Air
Southernwood (*Artemisia abrotanum*); perennial	—	SU	Green foliage	Air
Starflower (*Scabiosa stellata*); annual	S	SU	Tan seed heads	Air
Strawflower (*Helichrysum bracteatum*); annual	S	SU	White, pink, salmon, red, or yellow flowers	Air

KEY		
S = start from seed	I = best started indoors	SH = part shade
C = start from cutting	SU = needs full sun	M = extra moisture

Plant	Easy to Start from Seed or Cutting	Growing Requirements	Color When Dried	Best Drying Method
Sunflower (*Helianthus* spp.); annual	S	SU	Yellow or brown flowers	Air; oven
Swan river everlasting (*Helipterum manglesii*); annual	S	SU	Pink or white flowers	Air
Sweet Annie (*Artemisia annua*); annual	S, I	SU	Green foliage; gold flowers	Air
Sweet bay (*Laurus nobilis*); tender perennial	—	SU	Green leaves	Air
Sweet fern (*Comptonia peregrina*); shrub	—	SU	Green leaves	Air
Tall gayfeather (*Liatris scariosa*); perennial	S, I	SU	Mauve flowers	Air
Teasel (*Dipsacus fullonum*); biennial	—	SU, M	Green to brown seedpods	Air
Unicorn flower (*Proboscidea louisianica*); annual	S	M	Brown seedpods	Air
Veronica (*Veronica* spp.); annual or perennial	—	SU	Pink or blue flowers	Air
Viper's bugloss (*Echium vulgare*); biennial	—	SU	True blue flowers	Air
Wheat (*Triticum aestivum*); annual	S	SU	Green or beige seed heads	Air
Winged everlasting (*Ammobium alatum*); annual	S	SU	Pure white flowers	Air
Wisterias (*Wisteria* spp.); woody vine	—	SU	Lavender flowers	Air; silica
Yarrow, 'Moonshine' (*Achillea* × 'Moonshine'); perennial	S, I	SU	Gold flowers	Air
Yellow flag (*Iris pseudacorus*); perennial	—	SU, M	Brown seedpods	Air
Zinnia, 'Border Beauty' (*Zinnia elegans* 'Border Beauty'); annual	S	SU	Rose flowers	Air; silica

KEY

S = start from seed   I = best started indoors   SH = part shade
C = start from cutting   SU = needs full sun   M = extra moisture

Many new houses do not have attics, which is too bad because an attic is the ideal drying spot. If you don't have an attic, select the warmest, darkest, driest part of your home; perhaps the rafters of a garage in summer, a furnace room, or even a closet with the door ajar so air can circulate.

Oven Dehydration

If you want to try this method of drying, you don't need special equipment like a free-standing dehydrator. I use my oven to dry some large flowers, fruits, and vegetables. For drying peonies, large open roses, sunflowers, and citrus slices, I prefer oven-drying to any other method. I also dry apples and pomegranate shells this way and am experimenting with more materials all the time.

To dry flowers in the oven, place them faceup on the oven racks. Set the temperature to 175°F

and turn on the exhaust fan. (If you don't have an exhaust fan, leave the oven door cracked open.) Allow the flowers to dry for three to ten hours or more. The number of flowers you are drying at the same time, their size, and their moisture content will all determine the timing. Peonies and roses dry much faster than sunflowers, whose brown centers are dense with moisture. Petals dry much faster than thicker sepals and stems: If you get impatient and turn up the oven temperature too high (as I have done), the petals will burn before the center has a chance to lose its moisture.

Since all materials shrink as they dry, unless the flowers are large, they will become small enough to fall through the wires of the oven rack. Try a plain piece of rustproof window screening on top of your oven racks to hold smaller flowers. You can also try using a cake rack, but it may leave brown lines on the bottom of your flowers (mine did).

To dry citrus and apple slices in the oven, I place them on a cookie sheet covered with waxed paper, freezer paper, or parchment, turning them once during the drying process. This method is a little slower than drying on a rack since dry, warm air is not constantly circulating around the bottom of the slice.

To retain best color, remove fruits or flowers from the oven before they are 100 percent dry—keep a close eye on them to make sure they don't brown. Then let them continue drying at room temperature. The top of a refrigerator is a good spot to let a rack finish drying because in most refrigerators the warm-air exhaust comes out the back of the unit and flows over the top, which will hasten the drying process.

During the winter, I set small racks on top of my old-fashioned radiators to let fruits and flowers finish their drying. Use your ingenuity to find a warm, dry spot to finish off the drying process.

Pressing

The conditions for pressing are the same as for other methods of drying: dark, warm, dry, and fast. *Dark* is implicit in this method because once in a flower press or heavy book, no light touches the plant material. (If you're only pressing a few small flowers, you can use a heavy book; for anything more, I recommend a flower press.) *Warm* and *dry* refer to the atmosphere of the room in which you store the press–the surrounding air wicks out the moisture from the pressing paper. *Fast* can best be described by these tips:

1. Don't crowd the flowers on a page; leave an inch or more in all directions around flowers. Flowers will dry faster the fewer there are on a page and the fewer pages in a press.

2. Beware of thick flowers like roses. They will take much longer to dry than thin flowers like buttercups, and they may mildew before they dry. For best color, remove the petals from a rose or other thick

flower and press each petal and the leaves and sepals separately. If you are patient, you can re-form a fair approximation of the flower when you make a pressed-flower picture. If you lack patience as I do, use the petals as colorful entities unto themselves.

3. As the moisture evaporates, the pressure on the flowers will lessen, slowing down the drying process, so each day for about a week, retighten the wing nuts on your flower press. As you retighten the press, the plant material will maintain excellent contact with the absorbent paper.

4. Use only a smooth (unembossed), highly absorbent paper, like blotter paper or nonsmearing newsprint. Do not use book paper that is shiny and smooth; it has been coated with a substance that will hinder absorption.

5. For fastest and best pressing, change the paper after three days. Open the press and transfer all of the flowers one by one to dry paper. Run a paring knife under flowers to loosen them and use a tweezers to pick them up. Close the press and tighten the wing nuts. When you change the paper in this way, you shorten the drying time by almost three-quarters, producing outstanding color in the finished flowers. Of all the special tips on pressing, this is the most important!

Desiccant Drying

Sand, cat box litter, and cornmeal can all be used as desiccants to dry flowers, but silica gel, a substance with the consistency of fine salt, gives the best results by far. It is somewhat expensive initially, but it can be used over and over again. I am still using some of the silica gel that I purchased eight years ago when I first started to dry flowers.

Use silica gel to dry flowers that flop by

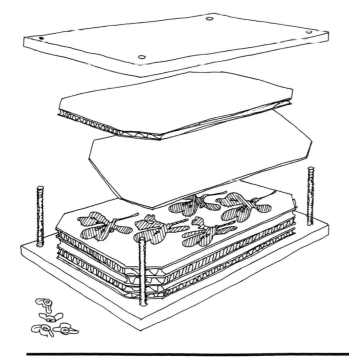

other methods. I dry lilies, orchids, tulips, daffodils, irises, carnations, and other delicate flowers this way. Open roses and peonies retain their petal structure and resemble fresh flowers when dried in silica gel.

Each container of silica gel comes with instructions for its use. The basic process is to cut the flower stems as short as possible and carefully bury the flower in the silica gel: Use an airtight, lidded container like a plastic refrigerator container or a cookie tin. Spoon a 1- to 2-inch layer of silica gel on the bottom. Settle the flower in the silica gel and spoon more of the granules all around it, building up gradually until you reach the top. Then cover the top with another inch of silica gel. Let it sit for about two weeks to dry.

All silica gel for craft use comes with little signal crystals mixed in. These are colored blue when the sand is dry. As you use the material over and over and it continues to absorb moisture, the crystals will turn pink to

warn you that it's time to dry out the gel. To do this, pour the silica gel into a roasting pan and bake it in the oven at 250°F for one to two hours. Stir several times during the process. You will note that the signal crystals return to blue. Remove the pan from the oven and cover it with foil, but leave one corner open to let any steam escape as the silica gel is cooling.

When the silica gel is cool or barely warm, pour it back into its storage container until ready to use.

I always wear a dust mask when I work with silica gel and strongly advise that you do the same. The dust particles from it may be harmful to breathe.

Freeze-dried flowers processed in expensive machinery look no better in terms of color and form retention than those dried at home in silica gel. The main difference is that commercially processed freeze-dried flowers have been sprayed heavily with a protective coating to prevent reabsorption of moisture. Most people who dry materials at home omit this step and are disappointed with their results.

Desiccant-dried flowers will reabsorb moisture if placed in a humid atmosphere. You can prevent this "wilting" in one of three ways:

1. Display flowers only in dry conditions. If you live in a climate where summers are humid, display these flowers only during the winter months when the heat is on and the house is dry. Or if you live in a warm, wet climate, display only when the air conditioning is on to keep the house dry. Store during spring and summer in an airtight black plastic bag with some moth crystals and silica gel added to the bottom.

2. Spray flowers with three to four light coats of a sealant. Spray the flowers individually before arranging them so you can reach all sides of the flower. Use a product like clear lacquer, heavy-hold hair spray, or a flower spray made for this purpose, like Design Master's Super Surface Sealer (available from your local florist or craft shop).

3. Display flowers under glass. There are many ways you can do this. One way is to buy a shadow-box frame several inches deep or an old frame with convex glass. Glue an arrangement directly to the picture mat. When the flower composition is encased in the frame, it will be protected from humidity and dust.

Or use an antique or new bell dome to display your arrangement. Purchase the dome first, then make the arrangement to fit, rather than the other way around—glass doesn't stretch to fit and interior dimensions can be very deceiving!

You can also find or make other glass-enclosed spaces like a glass-topped coffee table, a small medicine chest with a glass door, or a terrarium on legs. If you do decide to display flowers under glass, I still recommend spraying the flowers with a sealant for extra protection.

Microwave Drying

In general, I avoid the microwave for any serious drying. Flowers must be processed one at a time, and the timing is always tricky because it is dependent on the size and moisture content of each individual blossom. For best drying in the microwave, flowers should be buried in silica gel, and a microwave thermometer should be used to check on the temperature. As long as you have gone to the trouble of burying flowers in silica gel, why not just leave them in the gel until they are ready—a foolproof method—rather than gamble on burning your precious blossoms?

However, I do make an exception to microwave drying when it comes to poinsettias. (See "Dried Poinsettia Wreath" on page 128.) If you do decide to use your microwave to dry plant materials, remember to check your owner's manual for any special instructions. Manuals for many microwave ovens suggest that you leave a cup of water in the back of your oven when baking dry foods. Although this adds some moisture when you are trying to subtract as much as possible, follow the directions for your particular oven so you don't ruin it.

You can also use your microwave to dry lima and colored beans in their shells for decorative use. Process two or three at a time between two microwavable paper towels for 1½ minutes on high power. Remove immediately. Adjust the timing for your oven to achieve the best dried color of the beans.

CHAPTER 5

Projects
from the
Color Wheel

■ ■ ■

*T*he flowers are all one color but the wreath isn't boring. The various tints, shapes, and textures ensure an appealing display. A monochromatic color scheme is the easiest to produce, requiring the fewest decisions.

A Wreath with Fresh Flowers

The Color Theme

Pick a color, any color. Select all the flowers and foliage for your wreath or arrangement in that color. After you have gathered or bought your supplies and looked at them together, it's always surprising to see the variation among flowers that we refer to by one color name. The orange in my garden ranges from the red-orange of 'Tropicana' roses to the gold-orange of one of the Mexican sunflowers. (Of course, the wreath base, stems, and a few of the green leaves that remain provide additional contrast.)

Materials

Oval vine wreath base, about 22 × 16 inches, made or purchased (Here I've used catbrier for a nice thorny texture.)

Large handful of green sheet moss, dampened and wrung out

Assortment of fresh flowers and foliage in your chosen color (Here, from top to bottom: lion's ear, wild raspberry foliage, cockscomb, Mexican sunflower, dahlia, 'Tropicana' rose, nasturtium, and 'Meidiland Pink' rose hips.)

Oasis Igloo foam

12 inches of 24-gauge floral wire

1. Soak the Oasis Igloo in water for 20 minutes. Remove and wipe the bottom of the plastic.

2. The Igloo has a hole in the plastic on either side. String the wire through the holes and tie the Igloo securely to the bottom of the wreath base, slightly off center.

3. Insert the tallest flowers and foliage first. This is primarily a vertical design, with the tall flowers shooting up through the center of the wreath. To give the arrangement some depth,

---

Making It Last

A wreath with fresh flowers and foliage is not meant to last forever, but you can increase the longevity of the fresh materials by following these simple techniques:

• Select flowers with a good vase life—ones that hold up well in water. In this wreath, the lion's ear, rose hips, and cockscomb should last almost two weeks. Although not shown here, carnations, lisianthus, and chrysanthemums are also long-lasting flowers.

• Strip off most of the leaves from the flower stems. Condition all fresh flowers and foliage before arranging. (See page 26 for information on conditioning fresh flowers.)

• Keep the stems short on the most ephemeral flowers; here the roses are placed near the bottom of the arrangement so the stems can be cut short. Hang the wreath in a shady or protected location, away from the sun and wind, and add water to the Oasis Igloo daily using a watering can.

insert several stems in the back of the Igloo, so they spring up behind the vine, and insert the rest of the stems in front of the vine.

4. Now add some of the shorter flowers at the base.

5. Tuck the moistened sheet moss in among the stems to hide the Igloo.

6. Add the rest of the stems. Insert several up into the bottom of the Igloo so the flowers point down, like the rose hips here.

*W*hat happens to lost mittens? Singles that dropped while the owner tore off on an important mission; pairs that were laid aside during frantic snowball making, retrieved by someone else at the late spring thaw? Surely there is a mitten heaven where all the strays wait to be claimed.

While you are waiting in vain for mates to reappear and owners to reclaim their lost property, use your personal collection of strays to make a mitten wreath.

Mitten Heaven

The Color Theme

The colors on this wreath are in harmony with each other. They may not be your first color choices in decoration, but they make a satisfying grouping. I selected these objects from the mitten pile because they all have a medium-high level of intensity; a pastel pink or mint green would disrupt the harmony.

Colorado blue spruce makes a fine background for this color range of red-blues and green-blues. Use a conifer with a more yellow tone, like arborvitae, to make a similar wreath using mittens in primary colors.

Materials

36 pieces of evergreen, 8 to 10 inches long
   (Here, I've used Colorado blue spruce.)
12-inch-diameter Hillman wreath form
Pliers (optional)
Assortment of child's woolly mittens and gloves
8 sheets of tissue paper or other stuffing materials (Recycle whatever you have on hand.)
22- or 24-gauge floral spool wire
Wire cutters
Assortment of small toys
4½ yards of yarn
Scissors

1. Divide the evergreen cuttings into 12 piles of 3 cuttings each.
2. Take the first pile, position it in a clamp on the wreath form, and clamp the stems tightly to hold them in place. If you like, use pliers to bend the clamps.
3. Take the next pile and lay it over the stems of the first pile and clamp it in place. Continue until all 12 piles are used in the 12 clamps.

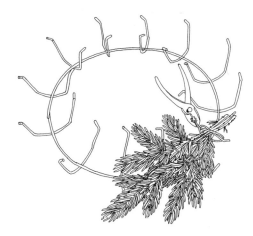

4. Stuff the mittens and gloves with the tissue paper or other stuffing materials.
5. To attach a mitten to the wreath, cut a 6-inch piece of spool wire and use it to tie the opening of a mitten shut. Use the ends of the wire to secure the mitten to an evergreen branch. Continue with all of the other mittens and gloves, placing them evenly around the wreath.
6. Cut a 6-inch piece of spool wire for each toy. Twist a piece of wire around each toy wherever possible and tie it on a branch. For the little car on this wreath, I threaded the wire through the windows; for the yo-yo, I wrapped the wire between the halves.
7. Make three yarn bows for additional color. For each bow, use 1½ yards of yarn. Starting with a 5-inch length, fold the yarn back and forth to make a 5-inch-long pile. Cut off the last 3 inches and use it to tie the pile in the middle.

8. Wire the bows to the wreath with small pieces of spool wire.

*U*se petite wreaths to decorate small spaces like the inside of this Hoosier cabinet. The apple mint flowers adorning the wreaths, combined with the mint candy decorations on the baskets, tell a subtle story of how plants are transformed into edibles.

Mint Match

The Color Theme

The color of the mints, whether actual candy or paper wrapping, is intense. The silver baskets and shiny ribbons command attention. A pastel flower like pale lilac spearmint would get lost among all this glitter and gloss. Within the range of natural colors, the apple mint has the brightest purple flower and the brightest green leaves. To create harmony of intensity, I used this herb to balance the basket decorations and harmonize with the other elements.

Mint Wreath Materials

FOR ONE 6½-INCH SQUARE WREATH:
16 pieces of dried apple mint or other flower or
    herb, each 3 to 4 inches long
28 inches of 16- or 18-gauge floral wire
Green floral wrapping tape
Wire cutters
Scissors
68 inches of wired ribbon, ½ inch wide
Hot glue gun and glue sticks

1. Bend the wire into a square that's 6½ inches on each side. Twist the ends of the wire together to hold the square. Wrap the joint with floral tape.

2. Cut off 16 inches of ribbon and set aside. Run a bead of glue on one side of the wire square. Take the remaining ribbon and glue it to the wire frame, shirring the ribbon as you go. Since the ribbon is wired on both edges, it will hold the shirring. Continue shirring and gluing the ribbon around the square, one side at a time.

3. Cut the remaining 16-inch piece of ribbon in half and bend each 8-inch piece to make two tails. Cut the ends of the tails on an angle and glue the tails on two corners of the frame as shown here.

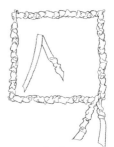

4. Glue stems of mint all around the square directly to the ribbon.

NOTE: The smaller wreath in the photo is 4½ inches square and uses only eight pieces of apple mint. For the ribbon quantity, double the wire length and add 16 inches for the tails; you'll need 50 inches of ribbon for the smaller wreath.

Mint Basket Materials

5-inch square basket with straight sides
60 inches of wired ribbon, ½ inch wide
Scissors
Thick white craft glue
About 60 mint candies

1. Cut off 40 inches of the ribbon. Set aside the remaining length.

2. Run a bead of glue just below the rim of the basket and glue on the 40-inch length of ribbon, shirring it as you go.

3. With the remaining ribbon, make a small bow for the top of the basket and tails for the two sides at the base of the handles. (See Step 3 above for directions on making the tails.) Glue the bow and tails in place.

4. Glue the mint candies in rows along the sides and over the handle. I left the cellophane papers on to add some sparkle to the design and to protect the mints from dust and prying hands.

*I*n France, an arrangement of flowers and vegetables or fruits is traditionally given to a couple upon their engagement to celebrate an abundant life together. Here we celebrate the bounty of the earth with a centerpiece for a summer party.

Earth's Bounty Arrangement

The Color Theme

Of the dozens of vegetables and flowers I could have chosen for this arrangement, I restricted the range to red, purple, and blue—three adjacent colors on the color wheel. The backdrop of 'Black Knight' butterfly bush, which was in full bloom for the party, inspired the choice. The garnish of purple basil and blue borage flowers on the cheese tray completes the color theme.

Whatever vegetables you lack in your garden will be readily available at your supermarket or farmer's market. If you don't have bachelor's-buttons, use any flowers in the color range, but look for informal flowers like these native wildflowers.

Materials

24 stems of blue bachelor's-buttons
24 stems of purple bachelor's-buttons
1 head of red-leaf lettuce
1 small head of red cabbage
2 small heads of radicchio
3 turnips
3 finger eggplants
1 red onion
1 bunch of beets
4 red bliss potatoes
1 bunch of radishes
Blue sponge-painted bowl
8 florist picks, 6 inches long, with wires removed
2 small jars filled with water

1. Condition the flowers in water for several hours before making the arrangement. (See page 26 for instructions.)

2. Start with the biggest vegetables. Put the lettuce and cabbage in the bowl. Part of each

---

Make Your Veggies Behave

If this is a centerpiece, to be viewed from all sides, place your bowl on a lazy Susan while working or keep turning it by hand so you view all sides of the container. If the arrangement will be placed against a wall, you need less material in the back and can concentrate on the front and sides. Never leave the back empty, however, or you will have a flat-looking, two-dimensional arrangement.

Treat lettuce, radishes, and herbs (like the purple basil decoration for the cheese) as if they were flowers. That is, condition them in water for several hours and leave them in a cool, dark place. This process helps leafy vegetables and herbs stay fresh out of water for many hours.

---

should protrude from the top.

3. Place the bunch of blue bachelor's-buttons in one jar of water and the bunch of purple bachelor's-buttons in the other jar. Nestle the jars of flowers amidst the lettuce and cabbage.

4. Now add the other vegetables, hiding the jars. First, stick a florist pick in the end of each eggplant, and in the potatoes and onion. Now you have nice secure "stems" to work with. You can stick them in the cabbage or lettuce to hold them in place. Note that each type of vegetable or flower is grouped together with its own kind. The beets are kept together in a bunch. Most of the leaves are cut off, but some leaves are kept to anchor the beets in the bowl. The radishes are kept together in a bunch with the leaves tucked between other items.

*D*on't just decorate a basket—create one from a hat without the work of basket weaving. Line the inside with a small plastic bowl, and you have an unusual plant container or vase for fresh flowers. Or stuff the basket with a bag of homemade goodies for any gift occasion, use it in a spare room to hold personal toiletries, or give it to a girl for her jewelry.

Hat Basket

The Color Theme

I started with a wonderful Panama straw hat in vibrant purple-red. For the decorations, I chose colors adjacent to the hat color on the color wheel, going clockwise for the red, orange, and yellow buttons and counterclockwise for the deep purple clasp. Keep in mind to use all adjacent colors and you can't go wrong.

Materials

Good-quality wide-brimmed straw hat in a hot color (The straw must be flexible enough to bend easily.)
Embroidery needle
Embroidery thread for sewing
2 matching buttons, 1½ inches in diameter
1 whole hank of embroidery thread for the clasp
4 matching buttons, ½ inch in diameter
36 additional buttons in various shapes and sizes
Scissors
Small plastic container, 6 inches in diameter and 3 inches deep (optional)

1. Thread the needle with unseparated embroidery thread, as it comes from the pack.

2. Using the needle and the embroidery thread sew on the two 1½-inch buttons opposite each other on the edges of the hat brim, as shown below.

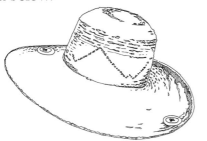

> ### Hat Tricks
>
> Use this same technique to decorate a hat basket in any color combination and for any occasion. If you have a blue hat, choose an adjacent color scheme of greens and yellows or greens and purples; that is, any two or more colors that lie next to blue on the color wheel in either direction. Instead of a basket splashed with hot colors, your blue basket can look as cool as a Maine lake.
>
> For a Christmas centerpiece, trim a white hat with gold buttons and a gold thread clasp, and fill the lined basket with fresh berried greens.

3. Turn the hat upside down. Take the whole hank of embroidery thread and remove one of the two paper bands holding the thread together. Slide the remaining band to the middle of the hank. Each end of the hank forms a loop. Put one loop over one button, then draw up the other side of the hat and put the second loop over the second button. The embroidery thread hank holds the basket together, but it can be easily "unbuttoned" for ease of sewing or filling the basket, and then "rebuttoned."

4. Take the four ½-inch-diameter buttons and sew one button 1½ inches above the clasp button and one 1½ inches below the clasp button on one side of the hat brim. Repeat on the other side of the brim with the remaining two ½-inch buttons.

5. Divide the 36 remaining buttons in two piles, keeping sizes and shapes approximately equal. Sew them on the inside of the hat-basket brim in random fashion, leaving approximately equal space between them.

6. If you'll be using the basket for a fresh plant or arrangement, line the hat basket with the plastic container.

*W*hen rice and seeds are outlawed at weddings, throw dried rose petals instead. Bedeck a simple pink fireside basket with roses for the flower girl to strew before the steps of the bride. Or the entire composition could be placed in the bride's home as a welcome for guests. The contents of the basket are part of the decoration.

Gather Ye Rosebuds

The Color Theme

Weddings and other romantic occasions seem to blend naturally with a monochromatic color scheme, and roses blend naturally with the color pink. I used all the tints and shades of red I could gather, from palest pink to deepest wine, with emphasis on the lighter end of the scale.

Not every bloom has to "match." I have saved these petals from climbers, shrub and tea roses, and floribundas; from my own garden, florist's bouquets, and boutonnieres. These are not my best, fanciest dried roses but petals, half blossoms, and blooms faded beyond their prime. The only things they have in common are the genus *Rosa* and the hints of color remaining.

Materials

2 or more cups of dried roses and rose petals
2 small pieces of dried fern or 2 dried rose
   leaves
2¾ yards of pale pink wired ribbon
2¾ yards of cream-color lace ribbon
5 inches of 22-gauge wire
Large pink or white basket (The one here is 14
   inches long.)
Hot glue gun and glue sticks, or thick white
   craft glue
Scissors

1. Cut 2 yards of the pink ribbon and 2 yards of the lace ribbon. Lay the lace ribbon on top of the pink ribbon and make a bow, keeping the lace on top. Secure the bow in the middle with the 22-gauge wire. (See page 150 for bow-making instructions.)

2. Glue the bow onto the handle 3 inches up from where it joins the basket.

3. Take the remaining ¾ yards of the pink and lace ribbons and lay the lace ribbon on top of the pink ribbon. Leaving a tail of about 3 inches, glue the ribbons to one end of the handle. Loosely wrap the ribbons around the handle, as shown in the photo, and glue them in place at the other end.

4. Pour the dried roses and rose petals into the basket in a pile, reserving the nicest 2 roses.

5. Glue one of the reserved roses on each end of the handle and accent each with a small piece of fern or a dried rose leaf.

*I*n your stash of old baskets, you probably have more than one that is too homely to reuse but too "good" to throw away. The basket shown here was retrieved from the bottom of my discard pile. It had red cardboard hearts and initials (not mine) glued on; some stenciling and dusty ribbon completed the look. I no longer recall the circumstances under which it entered my happy home. Since the structure was sound and the shape pleasing, it was ripe for a floral disguise.

A Basket Disguise

The Color Theme

Any pure hue with sufficient white added to it becomes a "tint" or pastel of that hue. With white added, red becomes pink, blue becomes baby blue, and purple becomes pale lavender. As more and more white is added to hues, the more similar the colors become to each other because the element of white is present in all. They all move in harmony because they contain more white than their base colors. Mix pastels together as you wish and you are guaranteed a pleasing and serene combination.

Some varieties of flowers grow in pastel colors. Choose pastel shades of strawflowers, statice, and larkspur. Other dried flowers are pastel because they have lost some of their fresh-grown intensity. The green eucalyptus leaves and the green amaranth here are both somewhat faded. With a pastel arrangement, you can mix true and faded colors as long as one element doesn't stand out as more intense.

1. Remove any old decorations from the basket.

2. Swish the basket in sudsy water if dusty and let dry.

3. Cut the flower and foliage stems very short.

4. Put the basket on the lazy Susan, if desired, for ease of turning as you work. Start at the bottom of the basket with the largest flower, gluing on one flower at a time in a ring around the basket. For the most effective disguise, leave no gaps between flowers.

5. Continue going up the basket and encircling with different flowers. Some spiky flowers like larkspur can be cut in pieces and glued flat to the basket.

6. You can glue flowers or leaves on the handle to complete the project.

Materials

4 or more varieties of dried flowers and/or leaves in pastel shades (Quantities needed depend on the size of the basket and the size of the flowers you choose—large strawflowers make the work go quickly; small globe amaranths on the rim take more flowers and more time.)

Small to medium-size ugly basket

Pruning shears or scissors

Hot glue gun and glue sticks, or thick white craft glue

Lazy Susan (optional)

F or greatest color impact, mass flower heads together. Without so much as a green leaf interrupting the sea of color, these flowers have a glow that lights up a space.

That's Intense!

The Color Theme

Intensity of a color describes how much of the true hue an object has; a hue that is unmuddied and brightest is most intense. The most intense colors have no black or white mixed in, no tinge of a contrasting color. Working with flowers to get intense hues is not as simple as working with paints. The first step is carefully selecting blooms with as pure a color as you can find. The second step is massing the flowers tightly in a container.

When you mass small flowers together, you create a visual excitement that one or two stems in a bud vase can't produce. Yet nothing could be easier than choosing one type of flower, cutting the stems, and stuffing them into a container of fresh water.

Even if your rooms are decorated all in pastels, there are always dull days when a jolt of color will lift the spirits.

Materials

12 or more stems of fresh flowers of an intense
    hue
Container
Pruning shears

1. Remove any leaves from flower stems.
2. Trim stems so the flowers will just top the rim of the container and not spread out too much. Shorten as necessary.
3. Add water and condition flowers as described in "Conditioning Fresh Flowers" on page 26.

Choosing Your Flowers

You can buy flowers for this style arrangement, or if you have enough, cut them from your garden. A third alternative is to transform nuisance flowers like dandelions or buttercups into eye-catching arrangements by taking advantage of their color intensity. Pick several handfuls of a plentiful wildflower. Singe the cut stem ends of dandelions over a candle flame immediately after cutting to prevent them from closing in one day. Arrange as described below for a spot of quick and easy color.

CHAPTER 6

PROJECTS FROM NATURE'S COLORS

■ ■ ■

*I*t's called honesty, silver dollar, money plant, pennies from heaven, or, botanically, *Lunaria*, and its seedpod lining reflects light with an opalescent sheen. When you peel off the outer shell and the seeds drop, use the lining in wreaths, arrangements, and basket decorations.

Moon Wreath
and Tiled Basket

The Color Theme

The colors of the moon shine through in these projects in shades of silver and gold. The wreath's green leaves represent the old belief that the moon was made of green cheese. The translucent honesty enhances the light of a votive candle placed inside the steamer basket, casting a distinctly lunar glow.

Moon Wreath Materials

4 large handfuls of dried green sheet moss
30 bare branching twigs, 12 to 14 inches long (Here I've used birch.)
10 stems of dried salal leaves
7 stems of peeled honesty, 8 inches long
White and gold dried flowers to fill cans (Here I've used strawflowers, golden drumstick, winged everlasting, bright star, and helipterum.)
10-inch-diameter wire wreath frame
24-gauge floral spool wire
3 miniature watering cans
Thick white craft glue (optional)
Pruning shears or scissors
Wire cutters
Hot glue gun and glue sticks

1. Spread the sheet moss out over the frame.

2. Tie the end of the wire to the wreath frame and wrap the moss tightly, going all around the frame.

3. Divide the twigs and salal leaves into ten individual bundles, using one stem of salal and three branching twigs in each bundle.

4. Lay one bundle on the wreath next to the wire spool. Use the wire to wrap it securely in place. Place the next bundle over the stems of the first and wrap it with wire.

5. Continue wrapping all of the bundles, placing them as evenly as possible around the wreath.

6. Glue the stems of honesty around the wreath with the stems pointing in the same direction as the twigs.

7. Fill the watering cans with little bunches of flowers. Glue the flowers in place, if necessary, to secure them, using white craft glue. (Hot glue doesn't adhere well on metal.)

8. Slip the handles of the watering cans over extended branches or use small bits of spool wire to wire them in place.

9. As a finishing touch, check that the salal leaves are relatively even. If too many seem clumped in one spot, snip off one or two and glue them to a bare branch where there is a hole.

(continued on next page)

Tiled Basket Materials

About 5 full stems of peeled honesty, giving 20
    seedpods
Scissors
Toothpick
Thick white craft glue
"Silver" steamer or fryer basket (freestanding
    on little feet)
White votive candle

1. Cut the honesty pods off the stem. Leave no stem remaining on the pods.

2. With the toothpick, dab glue on several pods.

3. Affix the first pod to the inside of the basket at the rim. Glue on the second pod, overlapping the first. Keep gluing on the pods around the inside rim of the basket.

4. Start the next row, overlapping the bottom of the top row. Continue gluing the sides of the basket, leaving the bottom plain.

5. Place the votive inside the basket, well away from the flammable honesty. (Never leave a lit candle unattended.)

Keep It Clean

Honesty (*Lunaria*) is a biennial (it takes two years to flower from seed) that blooms purple or white in May. When the flower drops off, the round seedpod begins to form and is full-size and bright green in about a month. Left on the plant, the pod continues to mature, turning beige and getting stained during summer rains. Eventually the outer covering and seeds drop in late summer or fall, leaving a much-stained and blackened (formerly opal) lining.

To protect the color, pick honesty in early- to mid-July, bunch, and hang to dry. Carefully peel off the outer coating of each seedpod on the stem when you are ready to use it in craft work, and you will have a gorgeous white pod liner. Honesty can last for years with the covering in place, protecting the fragile liner from tears and yellowing. Save seeds to replant in your garden.

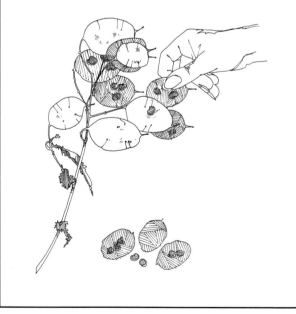

Gathering "Lunar" Materials

The moon wreath project calls for a fair amount of sheet moss and bare branching twigs. You can buy sheet moss fresh from the florist, and it will be green and pliable. Brush off excess dirt from the back and pin the moss directly on your wreath. It will dry in place.

Dried sheet moss is available in craft stores and in the crafts department of larger stores. However, it is often old, brown, too dried out, and crumbling rather than in true sheets. If you purchase sheet moss that fits this description, you may be able to revive it. Remove it from the bag and spray the moss heavily with water. If the moss is not too old, it may perk up and the texture will look much better. If you want to restore the color, mist the sheet moss with a mixture of water and a few drops of green food coloring. The moss will look most natural if you spray in an uneven pattern.

For most projects, you do not need whole sheets of moss—you can piece together any small fragments leftover from other projects, and no one will be the wiser.

When I list a material like the birch twigs, I am using what is available to me rather than insisting on a specific species. Use the clippings and prunings you find in your yard and whatever else you can glean on your wanderings. Winter and early spring are particularly good times of the year to observe the structure of trees and shrubs on your property and take note of what you can spare. One year when my flowering crab needed pruning, I waited until I needed bare branches for a project and was then rewarded with a surprising black, stubby wood to work with.

This year, with record snowfalls in Orwigsburg, Pennsylvania, I see that several limbs of the white birch in our center square have succumbed to the wind and weight of snow and ice. During the first thaw, I will save the town road crew some work by carting away what broken limbs I can manage. Eventually I will have the perfect use for them; until then, they will rest in my "savings" pile out back.

*W*hether fresh (the arrangement) or dried (the wreath), blue hydrangeas paint a vivid picture. Their varying hues remind me of the ever-changing sky.

Sunrise, Sunset

The Color Theme

The early morning sky awakens as rosy fingers creep along the horizon. As you continue to watch, lavender mist gives way to vast stretches of cerulean blue. Plan an arrangement around the colors of the morning sky using fresh blue hydrangea and other available flowers and fruits in rose and lavender. Select a pink glass bowl to enhance the color theme.

With sunset, a fiery orange ball sinks into the purple haze, and the blue-black night gleams with stars. Think of sunsets you have seen and the color combinations you remember. Here I've used red, orange, and lavender-blue flowers for the sunset wreath, and navy blue ribbon flecked with white for the advancing starry sky.

Sunrise Arrangement Materials

10 stems of blue mist shrub or other bluish flower, 15 inches long
5 stems of blue hydrangea
Large cluster of red grapes
6 red plums
5 stems of toad lily (*Tricyrtis*) or other lavender flower, 12 inches long
Pinholder
Pink glass bowl
1 to 2 cups of glass marbles
Flower food (optional)
6 floral picks, 6 to 8 inches long, with wires removed
2 tapers, 15 inches long (optional)
1 candle prong (optional)
1 candlestick holder (optional)

1. Condition the flowers as described in "Conditioning Fresh Flowers" on page 26 and wash the fruit.

2. Place the pinholder in the bottom of the bowl. Add the glass marbles.

3. Fill the bowl with water. Dissolve the flower food and add according to package directions, if desired.

4. Insert stems of blue mist in the back of the bowl, one by one.

5. Next, place the hydrangea, using three stems in the right front. Reserve the other two stems to fill in holes where necessary at the end.

6. Insert the cluster of grapes in front of the hydrangeas. Let the grapes spill down over the rim of the bowl. The stem can be in water to help keep the bunch fresh.

7. Insert the floral picks into the plums to give them "stems." Insert the plums on the left, in front of the blue mist.

8. Now add the toad lily or other lavender flower.

9. Check for any empty spots, perhaps around the back of the arrangement. Add hydrangea, if desired. If the flower clusters are too big, break some off and use them for a miniature arrangement.

10. If you wish to use the candles, cut one candle down by about 2 inches and place it in the candle prong. Push it securely down into the arrangement. Place the other candle in the candlestick holder next to the arrangement. The design looks best if the height of the two candles varies by at least 2 inches.

(continued on next page)

Sunset Wreath Materials

17 to 20 stems of dried blue hydrangea
20 stems of dried orange-red globe amaranth
10 stems of dried red plumed cockscomb
16-inch-diameter straw wreath base
3 yards of paper ribbon, 4½ inches wide, for wrapping the wreath (optional)
Hot glue gun and glue sticks, or thick white craft glue
Scissors
2 pieces of thin wire, each 8 inches long
2 yards of paper ribbon, 4½ inches wide, for the bow
25 floral pins
Floral tape
3 yards of gossamer ribbon, 1½ inches wide (optional)

1. If you choose to wrap the straw wreath base, untwist the 3 yards of paper ribbon and glue one end to the straw wreath. Wind the ribbon around the wreath as shown in the illustration below, overlapping the layers so no straw shows. Glue the other end down to the base. Trim off any extra. The ribbon wrap will show from the bottom and sides after the wreath is hung, adding a pleasing element of color.

2. With one piece of the thin wire, make a hanger for the back of the wreath by twisting a ¾-inch-diameter loop in the center of the wire. Then wrap the wire ends tightly around the back of the wreath form until all the wire is used and the loop is secure.

3. With the 2 yards of paper ribbon and the remaining piece of wire, make a bow. (See page 150 for instructions on bow making.) Here I have made the tails very short so they don't show and I kept the loops flat and overlapping rather than puffy. Make your favorite kind of bow and glue it to the top of the wreath.

4. Start pinning the hydrangea. Put the first flower head next to the bow, and pin the stem to the straw wreath base with a floral pin. Continue pinning the hydrangea around the wreath, each time hiding the stem of the flower cluster before. Hide the last stem under the bow and secure it with a pin.

5. Form the globe amaranth into a bunch and wrap the stems together with the floral tape 1 inch under the flower heads. Cut the stems to 4 inches.

6. Glue or pin the globe amaranth bunch into the hydrangeas.

7. Scatter the pieces of cockscomb around the bottom of the wreath and glue them in place.

8. For an ethereal touch, you can decorate the wreath with gossamer ribbon. Cut two pieces of ribbon 6 inches long and two pieces 4 inches long. Fold each piece in half and glue them in between the folds of the paper ribbon bow.

9. Take the remaining gossamer ribbon and tuck it around the front of the hydrangeas. There is no need to actually wrap it around the wreath. Just tuck it here and there amid the flowers. Glue in place if it doesn't want to stay.

Heed This Warning

To dry blue hydrangeas, you must wait until they are mature to cut them. If you cut too early, they will shrivel up and look dead rather than dried. To check for maturity, wait for the color to start to turn lavender or greenish. Also note a minuscule bud in the center of each four- or five-petal flower. This bud will open into a tiny floret, then drop off. You must wait until the hydrangea head goes through this natural process before it is ready to pick. Not every cluster on a shrub will mature at the same time. I generally harvest blue hydrangea from mid-August to early October.

As a bonus for waiting to cut, you can enjoy the bloom for about two months on the shrub and still have the dried flower for many years.

For a large, full wreath, corrugated cardboard makes a versatile backing. It's readily available from recycled packing cartons. You can cut it to any shape and glue or wire materials directly to it.

Dried canna or other large leaves like bird-of-paradise fit nicely into an arc or fan design.

Desert Fan Wreath

The Color Theme

In this wreath, the architectural leaves of dried canna and the red-brown stems of contorted willow produce some of the color range of the desert floor. Pink pepperberries and orange globe amaranth reproduce the colors of the setting sun on burning rock.

Materials

7 stems of fantail willow, 18 inches long
17 dried canna or bird-of-paradise leaves
36 stems of orange or red globe amaranth
2 okra pods, 8 inches long
2 okra pods, 4 inches long
7 stems of pink pepperberries
Pencil
Piece of corrugated cardboard (from an old carton) at least 10 ½ × 17 inches
Ruler
Utility knife or scissors
1 floral pin
Hot glue gun and glue sticks

1. Use the pencil to draw an arc 10 ½ inches high and 17 inches wide at the base on the cardboard. Cut out the arc with the knife or scissors.

2. Measure the center of the cardboard arc; mark the center top and bottom with a pencil.

3. Push in the floral pin at the top center of the arc, 1 inch from the edge. Spread the

prongs flat against the back of the cardboard to hold it in place and bend up the loop at the front of the cardboard to make a hanger.

4. The rest of the construction is all glue work. As you glue each item in place, hold the item about 30 seconds to make sure you have a firm bond between the plant material and the cardboard. Glue the fantail willow stems first, evenly fanned out around the form.

5. Next glue on the leaves, again in a fan shape. Cut stems as necessary to make the lengths even. Most of the leaves will reach right to the bottom near the center point. You may have to cut some short and tuck them in between the longer stems.

6. Glue on the globe amaranth in clusters of six, continuing to follow the fan shape.

7. With your fingernails, slit open the 8-inch okra pods; they will divide into four or five pieces. Glue them on with their interior sides showing for the lightest color. Glue the 4-inch whole okra pods at the bottom.

8. Glue on the pepperberries, covering any exposed stems or messy places.

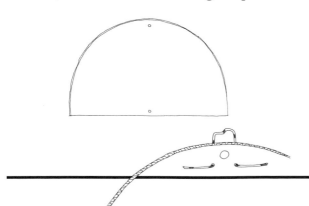

Drying Large Leaves

Florists sell (or can order for you) fresh, tropical bird-of-paradise leaves. You can also buy them predried, usually going by their botanical name, *Strelitzia*. Bunch canna or bird-of-paradise leaves in a rubber band, and hang them in a warm, dark, dry place for three weeks or until dried. They curl and twist in the process, making the final form most attractive. They are, however, very fragile, so be gentle when handling them.

*P*lace a feeder wreath where you can get a good view of the birds as they eat. After they pluck the seeds from the flower head, the honeycomb pattern remains to intrigue the eye.

Sunflower Feeders

The Color Theme

In the old willow tree where my sunflower feeders hang, woodpeckers have drilled six large holes in a massive dead limb. Bluebirds have nested there, then starlings. Last season the woodpeckers returned.

These sunflower feeders blend into the brown bark of the tree, yet stand apart from it. The tones of brown are as diverse as tones of the spectrum colors. Seen up close, the texture of the bark and the seeds add their own notes of variety. The cornhusks and bean pods remind me of the leafy season to come.

Materials

For one feeder:
Dried sunflower head
2 dried lima bean pods
Dried husks from 3 ears of corn
3 stems of dried rose hips or berries
3 or more pieces of dried grasses or grains
Ice pick or skewer
9 strands of raffia
Tweezers
Scissors
Hot glue gun and glue sticks

1. Gently poke a hole through the sunflower head about 1 inch from the edge with the ice pick or skewer. Enlarge the hole to about ½ inch in diameter. It's much easier to do this step with heads that are fresh, so if you can, pick or buy sunflowers before they dry.

2. Bunch the raffia strands and pull them halfway through the hole. Divide the strands in thirds and braid them, as shown on the right. Knot the braid at the end.

Harvesting Sunflower Heads

For a feeder, pick sunflower heads when the seeds are just becoming mature but before they begin to fall out too easily. To save seeds from being picked out by birds before you want them to, cover the head with a brown paper bag as soon as the petals fall off.

If you know in advance that you want to hang them, poke a ½-inch hole through the flower head about 1 inch from the edge. Cut the stem off completely to help in the drying process. Let dry on a cookie rack in a warm, dry place. (See "Sunflowers: They're Not Just for the Birds" on page 90 for complete instructions on drying sunflowers.)

---

3. With the tweezers, pick out some seeds to form the eyes on the sunflower "face." Glue on lima bean pods for the mouth, then cornhusks for the hair. Add the rosehips or berries and the grasses or grains for decoration.

While we often see jewel tones used in women's clothing, they are less common in home decoration or floral design. Using simple techniques, you can make a wreath that commands attention with its bold use of color. As with most wreaths, this can be hung on a wall or door or used as a table centerpiece.

A Gem of a Wreath

The Color Theme

Think of rubies, amethysts, garnets, emeralds, sapphires; imagine treasures of kings, emperors, maharajas. The rich colors tumble over each other in lavish profusion. On a humbler note, try massing dried flowers together in the wreath design. The hues intensify and seem to glow, producing a jewel-like effect.

Materials

Selection of dried flowers with jewel-like colors
(Here I've used 25 red globe amaranths,
20 purple globe amaranths, 12 roses,
3 peonies, 6 stems of plumed celosia,
6 stems of cockscomb, 12 stems of blue
and purple statice, 12 purple strawflowers,
6 zinnias dried in silica gel, 6 stems of blue
delphinium, 12 stems of purple larkspur,
3 dried pomegranates, and 6 dried pomegranates for the center of the wreath
[optional].)
Heavy-duty scissors or small garden shears
14-inch-diameter straw wreath base
40 floral pins
Hot glue gun and glue sticks, or thick white
craft glue

1. Cut the stems of each bunch of flowers to about 3 inches long.

2. Plan the arrangement of the flowers for the wreath. To do this, group the flowers in clusters on the work table, then make the clusters in the form of a circle. Move the clusters around carefully until you are satisfied.

3. All of the flowers are either pinned or glued to the wreath. Start with pinning first. Take the first cluster of flowers, like purple statice, and pin it to the straw wreath base, with all of the flower heads going in one direction. Then take the next cluster of flowers, like roses, and pin it to the wreath, covering the stems of the statice.

4. Continue going around the wreath, covering up the stems and pins of the cluster before. When you get to materials with very short stems or no stems, like the pomegranates, glue them in place. There is no need to cover every bit of the straw base, but you will So pin or glue some plant material to the inside surface and the outside surface of the wreath, not just the top.

5. For a centerpiece, place the wreath directly on the tablecloth or on a footed bowl (as shown in the photo) or cake plate. Put dried pomegranates in the center of the wreath for added decoration, if desired.

Working with Pomegranates

To dry whole pomegranates, select the smallest fruit you can find. Poke it through the blossom end a few times with a skewer to help the air get in. Also prick the skin in several places with a sewing needle through to the seeds. Put the fruits on a cookie rack with a tray underneath to catch any oozing juice. Then place them in a warm, dark, dry place for about a month.

A faster and more satisfactory method is to slice off the bottom and scoop out the seeds with a spoon. Rinse out the shell and set it on a rack to dry. It will take a few days in a warm, dry spot for the shell to dry completely.

If you buy pomegranates already dried and the color is less intense than you want, dip them for 3 minutes in beet-juice dye. (See "Dyeing with Plant Dyes" on page 21 for information on natural dyes.)

*T*he container is an important part of this floor arrangement. I have chosen a Mexican vase of mercury glass that adds a silvery glow to the pale flowers and completes the lunar theme.

Colors of the Moon

The Color Theme

If I asked you to make an arrangement in the colors of the moon, would you think of green cheese? Are you a realist who pictures the astronauts cavorting on moon rocks and craters of dull grays and black? Do you picture the shimmering harvest moon, luminous with an orange glow, hanging low over the horizon? Or do you think of the wintry silver and white crescent, with only a touch of gold? My floral interpretation of the moon has whites and pale yellows, but it must also shine.

Materials

Assortment of flowers in moonish colors of white, cream, and pale yellow (Here I've used from tallest to shortest: snakeroot, Queen Anne's lace, balloon flower, cosmos, zinnias, white and yellow snapdragons, crook-necked loosestrife, pale yellow marigolds, 'Casablanca' lilies, 'Auratum' lilies, 'Peace' roses.)

Large vase, appropriate for the floor, at least 2 to 3 feet tall

Pruning shears

Watering can or kettle of water

---

1. Add water to the vase and position it in the final site.

2. Strip all leaves from the bottom of the flower stems and condition the flowers. (See "Conditioning Fresh Flowers" on page 26 for instructions.)

3. Insert the tallest stems first: Here I put in the snakeroot, balloon flower, and cosmos first. Then add the shorter flowers: The roses had really short stems and I tucked them in last.

4. With a watering can or kettle, add additional water to the vase, within several inches of the top, so all flowers are well immersed.

A Floor Arrangement

Every house or apartment has a floor space that could use some brightening; in a front hallway, beside a fireplace, in a bare corner of any room, perhaps to hide a crack in the wall. I have a few vases that will hold tall stems of sunflowers or branches of forsythia to force in the doldrums of winter.

Your floor containers don't have to be expensive. One of mine started life as a 3-foot-high pasta jar. It's perfect for some bright red winterberry at Christmas or a few stems of flowering crab apple, heavy with fruit, in the fall.

Fill with water at the sink but make the arrangement at its permanent site, because these vases get unwieldy when filled.

If your flowers are very fresh and well-conditioned, this arrangement should last for more than a week. Keep adding water daily. To freshen the arrangement, snip out faded blossoms with your scissors or pruning shears, rather than try to drag out the whole stem through all the other flowers. A bare stem will stay well hidden amid all the others.

*T*iny spring bulbs and early perennials offer small
flowers reflecting the myriad colors of the soft
spring sky. From morning to darkest night, take your cue
from any celestial shade you see or imagine. Use both
floating and stemmed flowers to make an informal
arrangement.

Starry Night

The Color Theme

April Fools' Day is synonymous with "Pansy Planting Day" in my garden. The blues and violets of the pansy faces enhance the ever-expanding collection of golden daffodils.

This arrangement uses all the small blue flowers you can find. Once you get in a "blue mood," you may find yourself, as I have, changing some of your garden designs so next year you will have even more variety. From true blue, expand to lavender and purple to capture the feel of the spring night sky. I've also added some white "stars" to shine.

Materials

Assortment of blue and purple flowers (Here I've used pansies, forget-me-nots, squill, iris, and anemones.)

White flowers, such as baby's-breath, fresh or dried (optional)

Glass or crystal bowl with three glass vases (See "Tips for a Perfect Starry Night" on the right.)

Pruning shears

1. This is a very informal arrangement. Add water to the bowl and three vases.

2. Select six perfect pansies or other flowers to float, and condition the flowers as described in "Conditioning Fresh Flowers" on page 26. Cut stems to ½ inch and float them in the bowl.

3. Arrange other flowers in the three vases. Keep stems fairly short, since most of the flowers are small and you want to be able to see the floating flowers as well as the vase arrangements. Short flowers will support each other in the vases and need no other mechanical props. Put the biggest flowers in the vases first, the smallest flowers next.

Tips for a Perfect Starry Night

Here are some suggestions to help you create your own piece of night sky:

Spring flower combinations. Wild violets or creeping phlox can float happily in a crystal bowl or glass dish. Individual flowers of the iris family—especially the smaller Dutch, Japanese, or Siberian varieties—can either float or be part of the vase arrangements. In mid-spring, use hyacinths, camass, or Virginia bluebells as part of your arrangement.

Mix in white "stars" for an evening sky—fresh or dried white baby's-breath for the Milky Way, or tiny stars-of-Bethlehem for their individual shapes.

Vase construction. The pressed glass container shown on the opposite page was popular in the 1920s and 1930s as a way of displaying fresh flowers with fresh fruit. You can improvise a similar container by using a low crystal bowl and three stemware glasses. Simply position the three glasses in the bowl, add water to the glasses and then to the bowl.

Float and arrange the flowers carefully in each section as desired. This arrangement is best made in place so the glasses won't tip in transit. For further security, use small pieces of floral clay to attach the glasses to the bowl. However, be aware that the clay may be hard to remove should you want to deconstruct.

Look for odd pieces of decorative stemware, especially colored glass, at flea markets and yard sales. The glasses don't need to match to be attractive in combination.

4. If you are using white flowers for stars, add them to the vases last.

*I*f you want to decorate using the blue-green color range but are stumped by the dearth of natural aqua in real flowers, construct a still life of precious and found objects. This is one project where the flowers are not the feature; the overall construction is.

Colors of the Sea—A Still Life

The Color Theme

Dream of the colors of the sea on a brilliant day, when the soft greens and blues interplay with the dancing light. Think of the shadows on the water where the shallow reefs interrupt the white sand bottom. The variety of tints and shades is endless, but in my reverie, aqua predominates.

If you have never used the colors of aqua and turquoise in your home and don't think they will fit in, here is a lighthearted way to expand your horizons. Scour your house for every object in aqua and blue. Look not just among your beautiful home accessories, but for everyday objects in that junk drawer in the kitchen, your costume jewelry stash, button and sewing boxes, toy chest, and medicine cabinet. Search among your desk drawers and cosmetics. Part of the fun of this project is in noticing the colors of small stuff that you use daily, and combining fine goods with plebeian plastics. The coordinated colors of the individual objects give the still life cohesiveness. Don't forget to scavenge items from friends and family. Collect more than you think you might need. As you construct the still life, you will make a final selection of the objects that look best together.

Materials

Dried blue flowers like hydrangea or delphiniums (Here I've used only 2 stems of blue-green hydrangea, 1 whole and 1 broken in smaller chunks, and 6 stems of delphiniums.)
Many objects of different sizes and shapes in shades of aqua and blue

---

From One Plant, Many Colors

The blue hydrangeas come in many cultivars; some remain truly blue whatever the soil conditions and some turn pink if the soil lacks acidity. If you have one of the changeable cultivars and want it to remain blue rather than turn pink, try a light side-dressing of acid fertilizer in the spring, such as cottonseed meal; or dust with sulfur or work peat moss around the plant's base.

My favorite cultivar is 'Nikko Blue,' which remains true to color. Wait to pick the flower heads for drying until they are very mature. The color will start to change from summer brilliant blue to a softer violet-blue or green-blue. At this point, the flowers will dry well when cut and will retain their form and color.

---

1. Find an out-of-the-way spot where you can leave the finished construction to enjoy for a while. If you plan to use it for a dinner table centerpiece, know that the construction will live only until you reset the table.

2. Spread all the objects out in front of you and start placing the largest objects first. End with the smallest pieces. This is a process of trial and error, and your finished still life will depend on the objects you have found.

3. As you place things, keep the still life compact. Build with layers and overlap objects.

4. Vary the heights of the objects. If you need an item to be taller, stack it on something else like an overturned cup.

5. Distribute the colors; do not place all of the aquas in one spot—instead, break them up with darker blues.

*T*hese dramatic dried lotus leaves from a florist's shop retain much of their brilliant green. A "dried pond" is a contradiction in terms, but this arrangement retains some of the flavor and all of the memories of a water lily garden.

Colors of a Pond

The Color Theme

On a visit to the famous water lily ponds at Longwood Gardens in Pennsylvania, I wandered among the dozens of species of fabulous water plants, many with waxy blooms of white, palest yellow, lavender, and shades of pink and rose. No individual can hope to compete with Longwood, but I promised myself to plant a small water garden at the first opportunity. Maybe next year, or the year after...

When I imagine the colors of a pond, they are not necessarily the true colors, but my fantasy of what a pond can be. The blue of the "water" here is a little bluer than life. The green of the wall behind the arrangement is part of the green algae haze floating on top of the water. Because I could get no water lily or lotus flowers to dry, I used proteas, which are readily available from florists, and large white 'Zenith' zinnias from my garden. The white river stones are from the path to my barn.

About Proteas

The cut proteas come from South Africa, Hawaii, or California and there are dozens of different cultivars. To dry, hang them upside down in a warm, dark, dry place, the same way as you would air-dry other flowers.

Even though they may have a lovely rose or pink color when fresh, they lose most of that color in the drying process. They do, however, retain their unusual shape and texture. For this project I have tinted the dried flowers in a beet-juice dye to make them look more like fresh flowers. (See "Dyeing with Plant Dyes" on page 21 for information about natural dyes.)

Materials

Handful of Spanish moss
4 lotus pods on wrapped wire stems at least 14 inches long
3 dried lotus leaves (purchased, or air-dry your own on a screen)
4 dried proteas
3 stems of dried horsetail (If you can't find dried horsetail, replace it with 3 stems of cattail.)
2 stems of dried cattail
2 to 4 large white zinnia flowers (dried in silica gel)
18-inch-diameter lid from a round wooden cheese box or a similar low, round tray
Blue spray paint
Small knife
3 × 4 × 9-inch brick of brown floral foam
Hot glue gun and glue sticks
Wire cutters
12 white, smooth river stones
Beet-Juice dye (optional; see "About Proteas" on the left)

1. Paint the box lid or tray with the blue paint.

2. With the knife, cut off one-third of the foam to make a rectangle that is approximately 3 × 2⅝ × 7 inches. From the remaining two-thirds, cut an approximately 2-inch cube and a 1⁵⁄₁₆ × 3 × 9-inch rectangle.

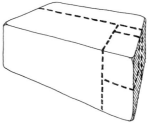

(continued on page 85)

Analysis of the Design

This arrangement is a series of circles, verticals, and triangles. The dried lotus leaves are the most dramatic round shapes. The blue "pond" echoes the circles of the leaves. The lotus pods and zinnias are also bold and round. To relieve the monotony, place the three horsetails and two cattails in vertical groupings.

The three lotus leaves form a triangle, as do the four protea blossoms, and the four lotus pods. If you use four zinnias, they can form another tri-angle, if you desire. You can see that the triangles don't all have the same number of elements (sometimes three, sometimes four) and the angles aren't all equal. Vary the angles and numbers to make the arrangement more interesting. In placing the materials, turn some slightly to the left or right, not all facing strictly to the front. This arrangement is made to be seen from the front and sides and should be placed against a wall because the back is rather bare.

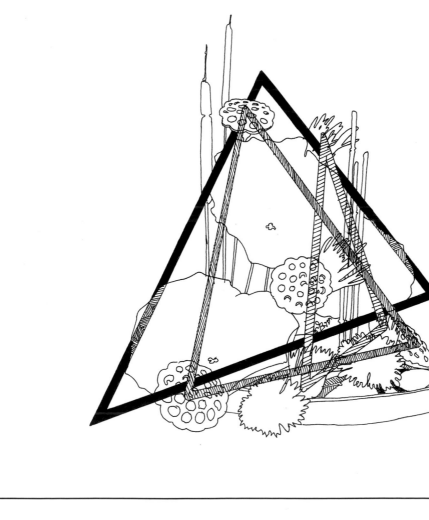

3. Glue the three pieces of foam to the inside of the lid or tray as shown.

4. Cover each piece of foam with some Spanish moss to disguise it.

5. With the wire cutters, cut the "stems" of the lotus pods. These are thick wire wrapped with kraft paper. Leave one pod with a 5-inch

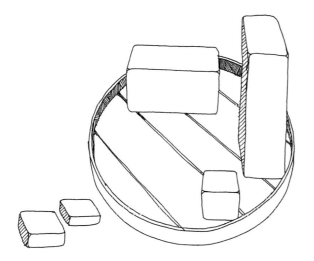

stem, one with a 7-inch stem, and one with a 14-inch stem, and remove one stem completely. Save the cut-off stems and glue them to the bottom of the lotus leaves and protea if they don't have their own.

6. Glue two lotus leaves directly to the two smaller pieces of foam. Glue a stem on a third leaf. When the glue is dry, insert the stem into the big piece of foam. The leaves should form a triangle. (See "Analysis of the Design" on the opposite page.)

7. Add the lotus pods in a triangular formation, with the tallest in the back. Insert them in the foam blocks, and place the stemless pod on the blue "pond."

8. Place the river stones on the pond surface, hiding the foam and stems as necessary.

9. Glue stems on proteas, if necessary, and add the proteas in a triangular formation.

10. Insert the horsetail in the small square of foam and the cattails behind the left lotus leaf.

11. Place the zinnias last, as if they are floating on the water.

*L*ike a floral topiary, this cluster of tulips rises above the carnation base to flaunt its blooms. Use this same design to create party centerpieces with other tall, top-blooming flowers like amaryllis and lilies.

A High-Rise Arrangement

The Color Theme

Although any container could be used, here the cobalt glass enhances the jewel-tone theme. I chose standard-size carnations in a rich burgundy and mini-carnations in the same tone, flecked with white for contrast. Brilliant ruby tulips are an alternate color choice. If you are buying flowers, to keep cost down, use standard-size carnations in place of tulips for the high-rise flowers, and use all mini-carnations to fill the base.

Materials

10 tulips, at least 18 inches tall
7 standard-size carnations
5 mini-carnations
Pruning shears or scissors
Flower food
Bucket of tepid water
2 cups of marbles or glass beads
Wide-mouth glass vase in a jewel tone
1 strand of raffia or a piece of narrow ribbon

1. Recut the stems of the flowers, with the tulip stems all the same length, and condition them in a bucket of tepid water. (See "Conditioning Fresh Flowers" on page 26 for instructions.)

2. Pour the marbles or beads into the vase. Add water, with flower food (if desired).

3. Stand the tulips one by one in the center of the vase. Tie the stems securely with the raffia or ribbon just under the flower heads.

4. Recut all the carnation stems to 4 inches. Place the standard-size carnations in a ring at the rim of the vase. Place the minis in a ring on the inside, letting them poke up slightly taller than the standards.

Planting Tulips for Cutting

The inspiration for my flower business started when my husband, an avid nongardener, planted a bed of cutting tulips as a gift for me. For the first time in my life, I could wallow in massed arrangements of tulips rather than stingily doling them out in ones or twos.

If you plant tulips in a cutting garden, select Darwin hybrids for the tallest, strongest stems; some Parrots for an old-world flavor; peony-flowered varieties for delicacy; and lily-flowered varieties for distinction. Select colors that will inspire unusual springtime designs.

Care of Cut Tulips

Tulips continue to grow after being in water and their stems often twist in the light. For this arrangement, you want the stems to be as straight as possible. Remove all leaves from the tulips. Wrap the whole bundle tightly in newspaper, with the top of the paper open, before setting it in the bucket to condition. Let stand at least three hours.

*P*lan ahead when you order seeds for your spring garden and add a few sunflowers for drying. Their cheery faces and hues of gold warm up a winter's day wherever you place them.

Sunflowers Shining

The Color Theme

Think of the colors of the sun, all of the sunrises and sunsets you have enjoyed, all of the glowing heat you have absorbed from Earth's star. We need heat to live and we complain when there are many consecutive gloomy days. The rich, golden hues of sunshine provoke a feeling of warmth in most of us. Research has shown that reds, oranges, and yellows make people feel warmer. Even the name "sunflower" provokes associations of heat.

Select dried flowers for this basket trim that reflect the colors of sunshine—gold, yellow, and orange. Choose any color basket; perhaps the leafy green I have here, or a buttercup yellow to further enhance the theme.

Materials

11 dried sunflower heads, 3 to 6 inches in diameter
5 dried gloriosa daisy flowers
3 heliopsis
10 safflower heads
15 'Sanfordii' helipterums
3 red cockscomb, broken into 10 pieces
13 salal leaves
Large magazine-size basket (Here the basket ends flare down, providing a platform for the decoration.)
Hot glue gun and glue sticks, or thick white craft glue

Three Ways to Dry Sunflowers

Here is a trio of simple sunflower drying techniques:

- Cut the stems, bunch three to five together, and hang them in a warm, dry, dark place.
- Cut the large heads and place on a screen to air-dry. (See "Air Drying" on page 29 for more information.)
- Dehydrate in the oven. Remove all the stems. Place head-side-up directly on an oven rack. Bake eight at a time in a 150°F oven for about eight hours. The actual length of drying time depends on the size of the flower head and the number of heads you are drying at the same time. If you have an oven exhaust fan, turn that on during the dehydrating process. It will help remove the extra moisture from the oven.

---

1. Glue the largest sunflower heads on first, three on each end; glue the two smallest on the top of the handle and the others on the rim near the base of the handle on either side. Note that I chose not to have the decoration perfectly symmetrical; hence there are 11 sunflowers, not 12.

2. Glue on the other flower varieties in order of size—the gloriosa daisies next, then heliopsis—ending with the small flowers. The

(continued on next page)

Sunflowers: They're Not Just for the Birds

Mammoth sunflowers grow 8 feet tall, and a ladder or a pair of stilts is needed to pick the head. Some of the new cultivars like 'Sunspot' grow only 2 feet tall with flower heads of 8 inches or more and are perfect for a small garden or for children to grow.

Helianthus seeds are big and grow quickly, and the blooms turn to follow the sun. Whether large or small, sunflowers make long-lasting, dramatic cut flowers, dry well, and also feed the birds. Roasted, the seeds are a favorite snack food for those who like their nutrition in a tiny but delicious package. Sunflowers are a perfect all-around crop for an adult or child gardener.

Pick for drying at several different stages for different effects. To keep the whole flower with petals, pick when pollen covers the outer half of the dark center. (See the illustration on the right.) Air-dry or dehydrate in the oven. For heavily textured seed heads to decorate wreaths and arrangements, pick when the petals (ray flowers) have died and the tiny flowers in the center have matured and brush off easily, revealing the whitish or black seeds beneath. For human consumption, let the seeds continue to mature on the plant. If left unprotected, the birds will probably pluck the seeds before you do. To prevent bird thievery, tie a brown paper bag over each flower head until the seeds are completely ripe, then cut the head and they will shake out easily.

salal leaves get glued and tucked into any bare spaces.

3. While I show this as a magazine basket, it is for people who place things carefully. If you're a magazine tosser, you'd better enjoy this basket with something more permanent inside, like a green plant, or keep it empty to highlight the decoration.

Sunflower Seeds in a Jiffy

When you harvest your sunflowers for crafting, be sure to gather enough so you can toast up some sunflower seeds for snacking. You're probably familiar with the traditional method of slow-roasting sunflower seeds in the oven: Place the seeds in a single layer on a cookie sheet and bake in a 300°F oven for about 10 minutes, turning frequently to avoid scorching.

Here's a quick microwave oven method for those who can't wait to munch: Spread out the seeds in a single layer on a microwave-safe plate. Cook on High for 1 minute, then stir. Cook on High for 30 seconds and stir again. Cook on High for 1 to 2 minutes longer, or until the seeds are dry and slightly crisp.

The best way to store sunflower seeds is tightly covered in a cool, dark, dry place like the refrigerator or freezer.

M y favorite forest is not all muted browns and greens. Mushrooms spring up in tiny flashes of brilliance and colorful lichens ring fallen trees. I've tried to capture the variety of forest hues in these basket decorations and this dried arrangement.

Woven Basket Decorations and a Secret Garden

The Color Theme

When you picture the colors of a forest, hues of greens and browns predominate. Here I've taken a rusty egg basket and one of brown split bamboo to decorate with grasses and leaves in different tones of green. This tall, elegant Japanese basket can certainly stand on its own merits, but it is also a perfect base for additional woven decoration. I selected bear grass and lily grass rather than one kind of grass because they are different widths and different shades of green.

But the forest isn't composed of only somber tones in deep shades. Take a walk in the forest after a long rain, and you'll see not only the many-hued greens of conifer needles and the tans and chocolate of the tree bark but also the bright reds, oranges, and yellows of fungi sprung to life. Examine the minuscule red "British soldier" lichen marching on a bed of green moss or the tiny red teaberries hiding under a leaf. After just such a walk, I chose the dark brown bamboo basket, green moss filler, and bright colors of the dried flowers in the secret garden design.

Tall Bamboo Basket Materials

---

13 strands of fresh lily grass, each about
    28 inches long (available from a florist)
5 strands of fresh bear grass, each about
    25 inches long (available from a florist)
Tall woven basket (This basket is 16 inches
    high and 6 inches wide on each side; for
    the basket of your choosing, vary quantities
    of grass accordingly.)
Scissors

---

1. Look at your basket and decide where you want the decoration. In this case, I decided to weave two sections with an added decoration in the front.

2. Start your weaving at the bottom of one side of the basket. Grasp the bottom of a grass stem. This end is tougher than the top and acts as your "needle." Here I used six strands of lily grass in the bottom section.

3. Reach inside the basket with the grass and start weaving it in and out of the uprights. Pull as you go, leaving the last inch of the grass inside the basket.

4. When you come all the way around the basket, end with the grass inside. Clip off any extra grass, always leaving about an inch of "tail." Push the woven strands together neatly.

5. Now weave the top section. Here I intermixed rows of lily grass and bear grass, weaving 11 rows in all.

6. If desired, weave a different design in the front of the basket with one strand of grass. Find the center upright. Start working from the outside of the basket. Put one end through the space to the right of the center upright and put the other end through the space to the left. Continue weaving any pattern that you want, working with the two ends in turn so the pattern is symmetrical.

(continued on next page)

Weaving Tips

Try weaving with any tall grasses, reeds, or weeds. Always work with fresh material or material that has been soaked well to make it pliable. Pull the grass taut as you go. When it dries, it should shrink slightly and hold in place well without any glue on the ends.

Leaves and grasses have subtle differences in color on the two sides. You can provide interest by reversing which side of the grass you use as the "good" side.

Grasses and leaves generally taper at the bottom. If you start each row in a different place, you won't have all the thin pieces together.

Egg Basket Materials

2 fresh palm fronds (available from a florist)
Egg basket or other basket

1. Hold a frond by the stem end. Weave the stem in and out of the uprights, on one side of the basket, pulling gently so all the leaves follow behind. As you work, make sure that the individual leaves are open and flat.

2. Weave the second frond on the opposite side of the basket. Tuck in the end of the stem and leaves. The leaves will dry in place.

Secret Garden Materials

FOR THE ARRANGEMENT:
2 handfuls of green sheet moss
12 dried safflowers
12 dried wine-colored strawflowers
4 dried roses
12 dried globe amaranths
Sharp knife
1 block of floral foam, either green or brown
Basket about 7½ × 7½ inches, with a high domed lid
Scissors
Hot glue gun and glue sticks, or thick white craft glue

FOR THE LID:
2 pinches of green sheet moss
1 dried rose with leaf
1 safflower blossom

1. With the knife, cut the floral foam to completely line the basket from edge to edge. The top of the foam should be about an inch lower than the rim.

2. Spread the sheet moss out over the foam to hide it.

3. Start with the safflowers. Cut the stems to about 2 inches long. Insert them in the foam, ringing the rim of the basket.

4. Next add the strawflowers. Cut the stems to about 2 inches long and insert them in a ring within the safflowers.

5. Trim the rose stems to 3 inches long. Insert the roses in the center of the basket. The

roses should be slightly higher than the other flowers because the lid is higher in the center.

6. Add the globe amaranths last, between the safflower blossoms. Usually the stems of globe amaranth are weak. I prefer to remove the stems completely and glue the flowers in place.

7. Glue a small arrangement in the center of the lid, with the moss, rose, and safflower. Warn people against picking up the lid by this "knob." It is only for decoration. Open and close the basket by grasping the sides of the lid. The entire arrangement fits under the dome of the lid when it is closed. If you display the lid resting on the filled base, the viewer immediately gets the feeling of something hidden and secret.

Please Be Precise

This style of arrangement—low, close, concentric, and even—is often called a Biedermeier arrangement after the German furniture style of the early nineteenth century. It looks best if you are very precise with the placement of the flowers. Try to keep each kind of flower equidistant and at even heights.

Check after the first few flower insertions to make sure you can still close the lid. Adjust if necessary.

*C*olor raw wood with stains you make from natural plant materials. Use wild blackberries, wild raspberries, and blueberries to decorate a produce basket and a small fruit crate.

Berry Nice Baskets

The Color Theme

Your mother told you not to spill blackberry juice on your shirt because it would stain. It stains not only shirts, but baskets and crates as well. If you concoct a berry stain, you can spread it easily with a paintbrush. The stain transforms the neutral color of unvarnished, unshellacked wood into a lively base for other decorations. Use any natural color dye to get the effect you want.

When finished, the basket looks lovely filled with dried grasses or flowers. I glued on small objects to change the color and texture of the berry-stained crate, much like a collage. The "gold" here is mostly brass, or some metal plating.

Drying Wild Raspberries

Pick wild raspberry sprigs when most of the berries in the cluster are red. There may be one or two purple ones and a few green ones, too. Cut the sprigs about 4 inches long and spread them on a screen to dry. Keep in mind that the berries will continue to ripen a little after being cut, so don't wait too long to harvest them. The leaves will curl, exposing the silver undersides.

To use in later arrangements, leave a longer stem, bunch them, and hang them to dry in a warm, dry, dark place.

Produce Basket Materials

16 sprigs of dried wild raspberry
½ cup of blackberry dye
½-peck basket, new or old
Paintbrush
Hot glue gun and glue sticks, or thick white craft glue

1. Make blackberry dye according to the directions on page 21.
2. Wipe off any dust or dirt from the basket.
3. With the paintbrush and berry dye, paint the dye on the basket. Leave the crosspieces and the rim in the basket's natural color, if desired. Let dry.
4. Glue the sprigs of dried wild raspberry to the rim of the basket. To do this, glue the first sprig horizontally, with the stem parallel to the rim. Glue on the next sprig with the berries covering the first stem, and continue in this manner until the rim is completely covered.

Berry Crate Materials

Paintbrush
½ cup blueberry dye
Raw wood crate, box, or basket
Many small found objects for collage
Thick white craft glue (Hot glue doesn't work well on metal.)

1. Make blueberry dye according to the directions on page 21.
2. Wipe any dust or dirt from the container.
3. With the paintbrush and berry dye, paint the container. Add two or more coats to achieve the desired color. Let dry.
4. Spread out your found objects. Make a plan. Decide where to place the objects: only on the front, all around, just around the rim, or in some other design. Here I used a random placement but laid out the design first so the spacing between objects is relatively even.
5. Glue the objects on the container. Let dry.

CHAPTER 7

PROJECTS FOR YOUR HOME

■ ■ ■

A bold fabric with large peony-like blossoms inspires dried flower decorations with the same colors and mass. Oven-baked roses and silica-dried calla lilies and peonies can stand up to this elegant summer slipcover.

Enchanting Circle
and Baked-Rose Basket

The Color Theme

The colors and pattern of this summer slip-cover remind me of a water garden. I wanted to create a floral impression of waterlilies to harmonize with the nature of the fabric pattern. I chose flowers, foliage, and colors that would enhance the impression of water.

I didn't try to match the teal green of the fabric background, as teal is almost impossible to find in a naturally dried flower. In fact, the greens I chose, like the galax leaves and the foxtail grasses, are yellowish in hue. The overall colors of the wreath and the fabric blend while not being identical.

When you look at your own fabric for inspiration, don't strive for an exact color and flower match—that would be boring. Instead, look for some colors that are the same and some that are different to spark interest in your wreath.

The basket, with its two tones of green and two tones of pink, makes a perfect foil for the oven-baked rose decoration. You'll notice that it is decorated only partway around; I did this so the basket can be used to hold a trailing green plant.

Enchanting Circle Materials

5 fresh peonies
5 fresh calla lilies
14 fresh galax leaves
20-inch-diameter grapevine wreath base
2 stems of dried hydrangea
6 pieces of pressed fern or other green leaves
18 stems of dried green foxtail or other dried grass
Pruning shears or scissors
Silica gel
Paper towels
Hot glue gun and glue sticks, or thick white craft glue

1. Cut off the stems of the peonies. Dry the flowers in silica gel, following the instructions in "Drying Fresh Flowers" on page 28.

2. Cut off the stems of the calla lilies. Reach inside each flower and gently twist or cut off the yellow spadix at its base. Dry the flowers and the spadices separately in silica gel.

3. Dry the galax leaves in silica gel or in the microwave. To dry them in the microwave, put one leaf between two paper towels. Microwave for 45 seconds on high power. Remove from the oven. The leaf will curl slightly and the surface will be textured with bubbles. Repeat for each leaf, reusing the paper towels.

(continued on next page)

Choosing the Best Materials

In addition to the color, shape, and texture of the plant materials, I carefully judge their fragility. For example, never use dried hydrangea, bittersweet, or pussy willow on a door that is opened and closed frequently. You will have potpourri on your floor in no time. Place these fragile materials on an interior wall where they will not be brushed against, and they will reward you with a long and beautiful life.

By the same token, a basket decorated with dried hydrangea should be displayed out of harm's way.

4. Once you have all the materials dried and ready, it is a simple matter to glue them on the wreath base. Start with the galax leaves. Glue them on in pairs around the grapevine wreath base.

5. Next glue on the peonies and calla lilies, at approximately equal intervals around the wreath.

6. Glue the dried spadices back into the centers of the lilies where they will show up well to the viewer.

7. Break the hydrangea stems into small clusters and fill in any bare spots on the wreath by gluing them in place.

8. Glue on the pressed fern or other dried green leaves, then clusters of three blades of foxtail or other dried grass.

Baked-Rose Basket Materials

20 dried salal leaves
6 large oven-dried roses (Here 'Double Delight' cream flushed with pink and red; see "Oven-Baked Roses" on the opposite page for drying instructions.)
2 stems of dried hydrangea, broken into large and small clusters
5 small pink calla lilies dried in silica gel (optional; see "Drying Fresh Flowers" on page 28 for instructions)
Hot glue gun and glue sticks, or thick white craft glue
Pink-and-green woven basket

1. Start the basket decoration by gluing on the salal leaves. I've decorated this basket on the rim, about three-quarters of the way around, leaving one-quarter of the basket rim bare. Use smaller leaves on the ends and larger ones as you get toward the middle. Let some of the leaves trail partway down the sides of the basket, both inside and outside.

2. Glue on the roses, either directly to the basket or on top of the leaves.

3. Add the hydrangea with smaller clusters at the edges of the design and larger clusters toward the middle.

4. For accents in shape and color, glue on the small dried calla lilies. These pink lilies darken when dried, becoming a deep eggplant color.

Oven-Baked Roses

Rather than investing in an expensive dehydrator—one more piece of equipment to stash in a closet—use your oven to bake large flowers like open roses, sunflowers, and peonies. Pick flowers when they are newly opened and when all the dew or rain has evaporated. Cut off stems close to the base of the flowers.

Place flowers directly on the oven racks so the air can circulate all around. If you have an exhaust fan in the oven, turn it on, or leave the oven door open a crack to get good air circulation. Set the temperature to 150°F and check the flowers after 1½ hours. They will take 2 to 4 hours to dry completely, depending on how many you put in the oven and how big they are. (I sometimes bake as many as 12 peonies at one time.) The petals will dry first. Make sure the thick part of the receptacle (where the stem meets the flower) is almost dry before you remove the flower. Complete the drying, if necessary, in a warm, dark, dry spot.

Oven-baking allows you to dry large, open flowers. This method produces flowers with a strikingly different look than what you get from air-drying flowers upside down. Oven-baked flowers look much larger and more open after drying. But this technique works only with large flowers, which won't fall through the oven rack. (Flowers shrink during drying.) If you want to try oven-drying smaller flowers, you can lay a piece of screening or a cookie rack crossways on top of the oven racks to hold the flowers. Be watchful for smaller flowers that may drop to the oven bottom and burn.

*W*hat if you have only a few flowers to make a grand centerpiece for a party? Perhaps your only garden consists of a terrace, a window box, or a few flowering houseplants. Gather groups of wee containers like old medicine bottles, china egg cups, cordial glasses, or eyewash cups and use them for individual flower specimens.

It's a Small World

The Color Theme

I started with favorite china given by an aunt to my daughter-in-law Emily. The most visible color on the old cream pattern is a Wedgwood blue, but tiny flowers of pink and yellow and green leaves contribute to the overall look. Rather than take the dominant blue color for the flowers, I selected a secondary color to highlight—the pink. For the centerpiece, I amassed old bottles available for very little money at flea markets and collectibles shops.

Materials

9 stems of fresh flowers in a color to highlight your china pattern (Look for small specimens to cut, even buds in color—not your prize dinner plate dahlias.)
Liquid dish detergent
9 small containers

1. With the detergent, wash the inside of the old containers to remove traces of medicines, dyes, or chemicals.

2. Remove the leaves from the bottom of each stem so only the bare stems go in the water.

3. Fill the containers with water and insert one flower stem in each bottle. Shorten if necessary so no stem is taller than 7 inches.

4. Place one container at each place, in a line down the center of the table, or in a square, as shown here.

Mix the Unusual with the Commonplace

For this arrangement, I pinched a small geranium from a pot by my front door and an African violet blossom from a gift plant on my sun porch to serve with other flowers at a special dinner. The other specimens include aster, annual poppy, zinnia, lisianthus, larkspur, snapdragon, and coneflower. The stems can be all the same kind of flower, like all pansies or all lilies-of-the-valley, or all different flowers. If using different species, keep them in the same color range so there is some cohesion to the design. This is particularly important when the containers are all different. There is enough variety in the texture, shape, and subtle color variation to make this an extremely interesting arrangement.

*I*f your wall-mounted soap dish is tired of the same
old perfumed cake, it's time for a change. Without
driving another nail in the wall, you have the perfect spot
for a new arrangement in a powder room. Find a small
dish for your guest soap and use the wall-mounted
container for the arrangement.

Something for Your Soap Dish

The Color Theme

Take your color cue from the background. Whether you have a vibrant wallpaper or a neutral tile, the arrangement should stand out rather then blend in and get lost. The tile here is an unusual shape and texture, but the cream color is neutral. I chose soft pastels and neutrals and was pleased by the effect.

You can adapt the foam and wire mechanics used here to many built-ins in your home. I've wired small cubes of foam to chandelier rings to decorate the light-bulb bases and to wall sconces for larger swag arrangements. Almost anywhere a bracket projects from a wall, you can attach enough moss-wrapped foam to have a base for an arrangement.

Materials

Handful of green sheet moss
Assortment of dried flowers (Here I've used
   7 larkspurs, 6 lamb's-ears, 3 globe thistles,
   4 poppy pods, 7 cockscombs, 3 Queen
   Anne's lace, 5 white strawflowers, and
   13 stems of blue sage.)
Paring knife
4-inch cube of brown floral foam
Soap dish attached to the wall
1 foot piece of 24-gauge floral wire
5 to 7 floral picks, 4 inches long (optional)
Pruning shears

1. With the knife, cut the floral foam to fit your soap dish.

2. Drape the top and sides of the foam with moss. Place the moss-covered foam in the soap dish, and wrap it with the wire to secure it to the neck of the soap dish.

Drying Queen Anne's Lace

If you hang this delicate wildflower to dry, the umbels will close up, hiding the tiny white flowers from view. To get nice, flat flower heads, cut the stems off and dry them upside down on a screen; or poke holes in the screen, put the stems through, and let the umbels dry faceup. Pick the flowers before they are fully mature to get the best white color.

---

3. The design shown on the opposite page follows an oblique line. It must be low enough to give clearance for the medicine chest door to open. Insert the tallest stems first, here the larkspur and lamb's-ears. Then work your way in toward the center, with some of the bolder shapes like globe thistles, poppy pods, Queen Anne's lace, and cockscombs. End with small flowers like strawflowers and sage.

4. If the stems of some flowers are thin and weak, like those of sage, take several together and wrap them with a floral pick, as shown below. Insert the pick in the foam.

5. If the stems of some flowers, such as cockscombs, are very thick, slice the stems lengthwise to make them narrow. Cut the bottom on a slant for easy insertion into the foam.

*T*his yellow and orange lithograph of rhododendrons in flower inspires a contrasting color
scheme, abundant with purples and tones of violet.
Although there are no other elements of purple in this
room, the contrasting scheme looks elegant. Look to the
color wheel on page 3 to determine the contrasting
(opposite) colors in a picture you want to spotlight.

Art in Bloom

The Color Theme

The Boston Museum of Fine Arts sponsors a yearly flower show called "Art in Bloom" in which floral designers create and display an arrangement in front of a masterpiece from the museum collection. The art and the flowers complement each other in color, shape, texture, and/or theme.

In my old stone farmhouse, there are four fireplaces and above each mantel is a modest painting or print. I love to make an arrangement based on some aspect of the picture and imagine what it would be like to be a part of the museum show. The flower design shown on the opposite page frames the picture on two sides, enclosing it without hiding it.

Materials

Plant materials in contrasting colors (Here I've used yellow verbascum, snapdragons, stonecrops, globe centaureas, heliopsis, purple delphiniums, pincushion flowers, bellflowers, Cupid's dart, and rhododendron leaves.)
6-inch-high container with a mouth at least 5 inches wide
1 brick of green floral foam
Paring knife
Floral adhesive tape or a floral prong
Pruning shears

1. Strip the leaves from the bottom of the flower stems. Condition the flowers and leaves. (See page 26 for instructions.)
2. Fill the container with a piece of saturated floral foam cut so it extends 1½ inches above the rim. Secure with floral adhesive tape or a floral prong.
3. To start the L-shape, take a tall stem and

On-Site Construction

Whenever you are making an arrangement for a mantelpiece, especially when you are highlighting a picture, work right in the final location. Spread a cloth on the floor to catch your droppings and discards. Place the container in its proper spot and begin.

Your final result will seem to be a natural part of the setting because all of the visual angles will be at the right height for the viewer. You can droop some flowers down over the mantel edge to break the plane of the mantel, again adding to the it-just-grew-here look.

---

place it vertically in the center of the foam. Take a slightly shorter piece and place it horizontally in the side of the foam. Add several more stems to the vertical, each shorter and of slightly different lengths than the first. It's best if these first flowers are thin, spiky "line" material like delphiniums, snapdragons, foxgloves, or stems of gladiolus rather than round flowers like daisies, dahlias, or mums.

4. Add several more stems to the horizontal, also slightly shorter than the first. Now that you have a strong L-shape, fill in the lower section of the design with other flowers. Use some of the flowers in the back and the sides of the arrangement. Add some at a 45-degree angle between the horizontal and vertical lines.

5. Select some small flowers (here I've used stonecrops) and insert them in the bottom of the foam with stems poking upward. This allows the flowers to droop down over the rim of the container and over the top of the mantelpiece.

The subtle coloring of an art-deco–style vase inspires the flower combinations in this arrangement. Since I've owned the vase for many years, I had stopped noticing the luminous quality of the glass and how the shadings of green, gold, and brown swirled into each other. Now, in making this arrangement, I wanted to view the vase as if seeing it for the first time.

Complementing a Container

The Color Theme

Choose a vase with an appealing color design. This design was made originally by an artisan who selected these colors. Examine every detail; notice each hue and tone. Now choose your plant material based on what you see. Either cut or buy the appropriate material. Fill in with foliage, branches, weeds, fruits, and vegetables. Let your imagination wander, but keep to the color theme of the vase.

Materials

Plant materials in colors coordinating with your chosen container (Here I've used foxglove, globe centaurea, and oriental poppies as the dominant elements. See "Be on the Lookout for Color" on the right for a listing of filler materials.)
Colorful decorated vase
Several small, clean stones
Shredded green floral foam (optional)

1. In a top-heavy vase like the one shown on the opposite page, weight the bottom by putting a few small, clean stones inside.

2. If desired, stuff the vase with shredded foam to hold the stems in place securely.

3. Add water, with flower food (if desired), almost to the top of the vase.

4. Strip the leaves from the bottom of each stem, and insert filler material first. Next, add the tallest stems. Continue to add the other material. I always like to end with the flowers or other elements that I want to be most visible; here it's the foxglove and globe centaurea.

Be on the Lookout for Color

If you choose plant materials with colors in mind rather than particular flowers, the most ordinary stems can become central to your arrangement. Here the still-green pods of the oriental poppy with their striking brown "velvet" tops provide a needed deep accent color. The silver-green underside of the artemisia foliage balances the pale opal-green at the top of the vase. I used seeded stems of sage and the weed dock as fillers, and buds of green santolina and globe centaurea to complete the arrangement.

If you make an arrangement of only foliage, it will help you to re-educate your eye to differences in tone, shape, and texture of green. Look for variegated foliage or leaves with red, yellow, or blue tones to add accents. Add bare branches for variety.

If you have one of the lovely green flowers like lenten rose, or Christmas rose, or the other green flowers mentioned above, you can build an all-green arrangement using them as the focal point.

*W*hether you have an authentic painted New England chest circa 1750 or a do-it-yourself painted dining room table circa 1994, an arrangement of dried flowers will enhance the pattern and colors.

Painted Furniture and Flower Decoration

The Color Theme

When the surface on your old dining room table is ringed with years of stains and you don't look forward to the effort of refinishing, consider painting it with a decorative pattern. Here artist Richard Snyder painted a lock-and-key design, inspired by a collection of old keys hanging on a nearby wall. The muted yellow, green, and blue of the central theme is accented by the black of the painted keys, then brushed over with a coat of glaze and matte varnish (all available at your local paint store).

The colors in the dried flower arrangement are soft, like the colors of the paint, but the style is bold enough to provide some drama.

Materials

Green sheet moss, 10 × 10 inches
8 stems of dried blue delphinium
8 stems of dried golden cockscomb
11 stems of dried golden yarrow
18 dried globe thistles
32 gold strawflowers on wire stems
18 poppy seed pods
18 salal leaves
Paring knife
Block of brown floral foam
Wide-mouth footed bowl (here 10 inches wide and 5½ inches high)
Floral adhesive
Floral prong
Pruning shears or scissors
Hot glue gun and glue sticks, or thick white craft glue

1. Cut the floral foam to fit in the bowl but let it extend ½ inch above the rim.

2. Press the floral adhesive on the bottom of the prong, then press the prong on the bottom of the bowl. Center the trimmed block of foam over the prong and press down firmly.

3. Spread the green sheet moss over the foam to hide it from view.

4. Insert a stem of delphinium in the center of the foam. Add the remaining delphiniums around it, keeping all the stems at approximately the same height.

5. Trim the cockscombs to about 8 inches shorter than the delphiniums and encircle the delphiniums with cockscombs, again keeping the stems as even as possible.

6. Keep adding rings of flowers in the order of the materials list, cutting stems as necessary so that each ring is shorter than the one previous and flowers are at the same height within each ring.

7. Insert the poppy pods next to last, placing them almost horizontally in the foam. Then glue salal leaves in between the poppy pods, adhering them to the sheet moss.

*T*his locust basket makes a fine repository for an
umbrella and cane collection. Although most of the
collection is decorative rather than strictly utilitarian, I
keep the flower design well away from the mouth of the
basket so an item can be removed without destroying
the plant material.

Neutrals Stand Out

The Color Theme

Black, white, and brown are not colors, strictly speaking, because they are not part of the spectrum. We call them and their mixtures—like gray and beige—"neutrals." In the home, a neutral color scheme of all beige, cream, and brown or all gray, white, and black can soothe and comfort. But if the contrasts are very intense—like stark black and white—and the patterns are bold, neutrals assume a distinctly modernistic feel.

In this sitting room, the decorative elements take their neutral tones from the buffalo-plaid and ticking upholsteries. With an absence of color, textures and shapes become more compelling. I want the plant material to follow the other neutrals in the room. If we add a vase of brilliantly colored flowers and a bowl of fresh fruit in the summer, the room undergoes a temporary transformation and the neutral tones serve as a backdrop for the color. You can choose any mixture of pods, vines, and grasses, 8 to 22 inches tall, to decorate your basket. Feel free to substitute materials in this arrangement. For example, you can use one or two large lotus pods in the center instead of the sunflower.

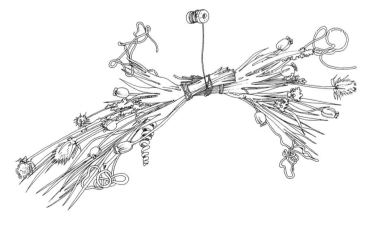

Materials

1 sunflower head
2 okra pods
4 stems of kiwi vine
2 stalks of mullein
10 poppy seed pods
4 teasels
4 stems of black-bearded wheat
2 sorghum stalks
6 pods of globe centaurea (and because I wanted a botanical pun, 1 coil of river cane to match the cane collection)
24-gauge floral spool wire
Wire cutters
Any large basket (The one shown here is 21 inches tall; this decoration is also adaptable to any hamper-type basket.)
Hot glue gun and glue sticks
Pruning shears or scissors

---

1. Set aside the sunflower head and okra pods.

2. Divide the other plant materials into two approximately equal piles.

3. Start with one pile and make a bouquet with the tallest materials in the back. Wrap the stems with the wire to secure them, and cut the wire. Repeat with the other pile.

4. Lay the bouquets end to end and overlap the ends by 4 inches. Wrap the bouquets together, as shown on the left, and secure tightly with wire. You will have a long swag.

5. Place the swag on the basket at an angle. Wire the swag to the basket. You should be able to thread the wire right through the weave of the basket.

6. Glue the sunflower head to the center of the swag, hiding the wrapping wires.

7. Open the okra pods and glue one on each side of the sunflower.

CHAPTER 8

PROJECTS FOR THE HOLIDAYS

■ ■ ■

*S*ummer annuals give way to a winter arrangement "planted" in a concrete container. The cut boughs will last for many months given some water or snow and cool weather. Match a winter door wreath to the arrangement and the pair extend the Christmas season.

Christmas Evergreens

The Color Theme

The enormous variety in evergreen colors enhances both gardens and arrangements. Rich tones of blue-green juniper and yellow-green cypress stand out against the forest green pine. The reddish buds of the evergreen lily-of-the-valley bush match the color of the rusty-red door. Red twig dogwood branches in the urn arrangement complete the theme of nature's red.

Hunt for variations in color of conifer and broadleaf evergreens when you are designing for Christmas. Not shown here but also of interest are the shiny green of the southern magnolia as well as the rust-hued undersides of the magnolia leaves and many rhododendrons.

Arrangement Materials

Assortment of multicolored evergreen boughs, cones, and bare branches (Here I've used white and mountain pine, blue juniper in berry, golden cypress, lily-of-the-valley bush in winter bud, bare branches of red twig dogwood, and one large pinecone.)
Outdoor container filled with moist soil
Pruning shears

1. Make this arrangement right where it will stand. Put in the largest branches first. Press the ends at least 4 inches into the soil to anchor them.

2. Insert the other branches and pinecone. I added the golden cypress last since I had the least of that and wanted to make sure its color stood out in the arrangement.

Wreath Materials

Assortment of multicolored evergreen boughs, including white and mountain pine, blue juniper in berry, golden cypress, and lily-of-the-valley bush in winter bud
Pruning shears
14-inch wire wreath "box" frame
22- to 26-gauge floral spool wire
3 yards of plaid wired ribbon

1. Trim all the evergreens to about 6 inches long. Set aside.

2. Turn the wreath frame hollow-side-up and fill the frame with the leftover trimmings, as shown below. Attach the wire anywhere along the frame and wrap all the trimmings securely inside the frame. Tie and cut off the wire. While this step is optional, it helps to keep the wreath rigid and allows you to insert extra stems directly into the wreath base to make final adjustments.

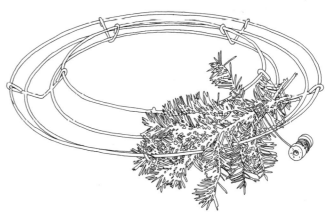

(continued on next page)

3. Cut a 6-inch piece of wire and twist it to the back of the wreath for a hanger.

4. Turn over the filled frame. Decide on your pattern. In the wreath shown on page 118, the bow is at the top and the greens are in clusters.

5. Attach the wire to the outermost ring of the wreath frame at the bottom. Lay the first cluster of four to six stems where you've attached the wire, with tips pointing outward and on a slant, extending 3 to 5 inches off the wreath frame. Wrap tightly with wire.

6. Lay the next cluster on a middle ring, next to the first. Attach the third cluster to the innermost ring. As you add clusters, cover the

stems of the previous cluster. In this manner, work up one side and end at the top.

7. Start at the bottom again and work up the other side of the frame, continuing to wrap clusters to the top. Cut off the wire.

8. Make a bow with the wired ribbon. (See page 150 for instructions.) Attach the bow at the top of the wreath.

9. To finish off the wreath, insert any extra stems where it looks bare, perhaps at the bottom where you started wrapping. These last few stems will be held in place if you push them securely through the other tightly wrapped greens.

Recycle Your Christmas Tree

If you use a fresh-cut tree for decorating at holiday time, don't discard your greenery trimmings. Instead, recycle the evergreen boughs by adding them to your outdoor arrangement. Use them as additional material for an even fuller, more lush look, or use them as replacements for any greens that are starting to yellow.

Your Christmas tree trimmings can also be used to make an additional arrangement for your patio. You can also use any leftover evergreen boughs as mulch on your perennial garden beds.

The Many Colors of Evergreens

While many people think of evergreens as being just green, the truth is that evergreen colors vary considerably, from various shades of green to blue to rust to gold. Here's a look at the beautiful palette of evergreens.

EVERGREEN	WINTER FOLIAGE COLOR
'Bar Harbor' juniper (*Juniperus horizontalis* 'Bar Harbor')	Blue to blue-gray
Blue moss Sawara false cypress (*Chamaecyparis pisifera* 'Boulevard')	Blue to blue-gray
Blue rug juniper (*Juniperus horizontalis* 'Wiltonii')	Blue
Compact oriental spruce (*Picea orientalis* 'Aurea Compacta')	Gold
Dragon's eye pine (*Pinus densiflora*)	Variegated
English yew (*Taxus baccata* 'Aurea')	Gold
'Fat Albert' blue spruce (*Picea pungens* 'Fat Albert')	Blue
'Francis Mason' glossy abelia (*Abelia × grandiflora* 'Francis Mason')	Gold
'Golden Gem' Japanese holly (*Ilex crenata* 'Golden Gem')	Gold
'Golden mop' Sawara false cypress (*Chamaecyparis pisifera* 'Golden Mop')	Gold
Hinoki false cypresses (*Chamaecyparis obtusa* 'Fernspray Gold', 'Golden Drop', 'Golden Sprite')	Gold
Japanese aucuba (*Aucuba japonica*)	Variegated
Japanese yew (*Taxus cuspidata* 'Aurescens')	Gold
'Mikko' Sawara false cypress (*Chamaecyparis pisifera* 'Mikko')	Blue to blue-gray
'Mother Lode' creeping juniper (*Juniperus horizontalis* 'Mother Lode')	Gold
Pfitzer juniper (*Juniperus chinensis* 'pfitzeriana Aurea')	Gold
Purple-leaf wintercreeper (*Euonymus fortunei* 'Colorata')	Purplish
Red cedar (*Juniperus Virginiana*)	Purplish red
'Red Mill' Japanese pieris (*Pieris japonica* 'Red Mill')	Red
Silver-edge English holly (*Ilex aquifolium* 'Argenteo-Marginata')	Variegated
'Snow Sprite' deodar cedar (*Cedrus deodara* 'Snow Sprite')	Variegated
Standish English yew (*Taxus baccata* 'Standishii')	Gold
Threadleaved Sawara false cypress (*Chamaecyparis pisifera* 'Filifera Aurea')	Gold
Variegated boxwood (*Buxus sempervirens* 'Elegantissima')	Variegated
Variegated winter daphne (*Daphne odora* 'Aureo-Marginata')	Variegated
Waukegan juniper (*Juniperus horizontalis* 'Douglasii')	Purplish

The mirror backing makes this wreath utilitarian as well as decorative. Hang it at eye level in an entrance or hallway or in a guest or powder room where friends and family can admire themselves—and you for your handiwork.

Hot Pepper Wreath

The Color Theme

Red and gold are a traditional combination for Christmas, but the selection of materials is anything but traditional. Dried yarrow is a natural bright gold, and the various reds of the dried peppers make a striking contrast.

Materials

Assorted dried peppers, 12 long, 10 round, 24 small
8 small heads of golden yarrow
Oval vine wreath base, 10 × 14 inches, or round vine wreath base about 12 inches in diameter (made or purchased)
Mirror ½ inch smaller all around than the wreath base
Epoxy glue
6-inch piece of 24-gauge wire
Hot glue gun and glue sticks

1. Fashion the vine wreath base to be a little bigger than the size of the mirror, then glue the two together with epoxy. I take the lazy way out and take the wreath to an auto glass and mirror store, where the mirror is cut to shape and is glued to the back of the wreath with epoxy.

2. Twist the piece of wire to the back of the wreath to make a hanger.

3. The remaining task is gluing on the decoration. Start with the large, long peppers and hot-glue them around the outside of the wreath base, with the tips all swirling in one direction. Then glue on the yarrow, on the inner circle of the wreath, near the mirror. Finish with the smaller peppers.

Drying Peppers

Pick or buy firm, unblemished peppers. Because weather is humid in the Northeast, I dry large peppers in the oven. Set the temperature to 175°F. With a paring knife, make a slit 1 to 2 inches long in each pepper to help the inside dry faster. Put peppers on a cookie sheet lined with waxed paper. The drying process takes about ten hours at this low temperature, and of course it depends on the size of the peppers and the quantity you are drying. Turn peppers over during the process to hasten drying of their bottoms. I switch on the exhaust fan to remove excess humidity from the oven. Remove the peppers from the oven when they are leathery, not brittle, and let them finish air-drying on a cookie rack.

Of course, if you live in the Southwest or in another dry area, the peppers will dry beautifully simply hung or put on a rack outside in the sun. Or if you own an electric dehydrator, use that instead of the oven; follow the manufacturer's instructions for use.

Red peppers turn a rich red; the round black ones in the photo on the opposite page were dried when they were still green. For a more orangey color, start with an underripe red pepper.

*C*rimson apples add the color of Christmas to an arrangement of winter-white fresh flowers. The apples support the flower stems without need for additional mechanical aids. If you add fresh water to the arrangement daily, it should last almost two weeks.

Apple "Punch"

The Color Theme

This arrangement sings of Christmas, with its variety of red tones. From the subtle pink of the alstromeria flowers to the warm rose of the tablecloth, the rich crimson of the local (unwaxed) Delicious apples, and the translucent glass handles of the punch cups and bowl stem, there is no doubt that we can celebrate Christmas here.

I chose a simple white color scheme for the other flowers to make the design appropriate for any occasion throughout the winter. The Queen Anne's lace (purchased from a florist because none grows here in winter) reminds me of snowflakes in this context.

Materials

5 pounds of unblemished Red Delicious apples
1 bunch of Queen Anne's lace
1 bunch of white daisy mums
3 stems of white or pale pink alstromeria
Glass punch bowl or salad bowl
Pruning shears or scissors

1. Wash the apples and layer them in the glass bowl, with their best sides facing outward. Fill in the center of the bowl, too, not just the outsides, to hold the whole construction in place. The apples should reach to within 3 to 4 inches from the top of the bowl.

More Apple Arranging

Here are a few suggestions to make your Apple Punch arrangement stand out:

• When you insert a flower stem into the bowl, put it toward the middle of the apple construction so the stems won't show on the outside of the bowl.

• To reduce the cost of the fresh flowers (this arrangement, as shown, has no greens or other fillers), substitute gathered pine or holly for one variety of fresh flowers, or exchange the alstromeria for white cushion mums or pompoms.

• Add 3-foot strands of ivy to the bowl, and let them trail down around the punch cups and refreshments.

---

2. Add water to the top of the apples. Do not fill the bowl with water first—the apples will only bob around and will never stay in place.

3. Cut the stems of the Queen Anne's lace to 8 inches long. Insert them around the edges of the bowl. Then fill in the center so the whole surface is filled with the Queen Anne's lace.

4. Cut the stems of daisy mums to 8 inches long. Insert them among the other flowers.

5. Add the alstromeria last. Cut their stems to about 8 inches long and remove most of the leaves. When cut this short, each stem can be separated, giving three or four pieces. Insert the pieces in the bowl a little higher than the other flowers.

6. If necessary, add more water so that all stems are submerged and add fresh water daily.

*G*ather some objects with a musical flavor, add some old rolled sheet music, throw in some fresh Christmas greens and a few dried roses, and place on a piano or entrance table for a long-lasting holiday composition.

Musical Composition

The Color Theme

Back to basics—green and red for the Christmas season—with an accent of brass. The red enamel of the purchased basket is an excellent foil for the other materials, and mirrors the color of the dried roses.

The choice of roses rather than holly berries for additional red adds interest but also comes from personal necessity. Although the landscaper who planted my two holly bushes swore they were male and female, they flower profusely but bear no berries. Rather than rip one out, I make do by adding other reds to the gleaming green foliage in arrangements. Find ways of substituting materials you have for those you can't find. Also beg, buy, or trade for plants you covet.

Materials

- 4 stems of holly leaves, 10 inches long
- 5 dried red roses
- 2 branches of pine
- 3 or 4 pages of sheet music
- 5 rubber bands
- Scissors
- 1½ yards of white silk ribbon, 2 to 3 inches wide
- Red basket
- Several music-related objects such as a metronome, decorative horns, or brass bells (Here I've used drumsticks and an old auto horn with the rubber bulb torn.)

1. Roll each sheet of music and slip on a rubber band to secure. I have folded one like an accordion for variety. Gather the rolled music together and slip another rubber band around all the rolls.

For Long-Lasting Greens . . .

You well know that greens in water last longer. You can hide small containers of water or soaked floral foam in the basket to hold the pine branches.

Holly dries well if it is undisturbed in an arrangement, and it still looks nice after several months. Try boxwood or arborvitae for other greens that work well without water.

---

2. Cut off ½ yard of ribbon. Tie this around the sheet music, hiding the rubber bands, making two streamers but no bow. Use the remaining yard to tie in a bow around the roll, on top of the streamers, as shown below.

3. Slip two stems of holly under the ribbon. Add the roses in the same way, just slipping them under the ribbon. Place this music bouquet inside the basket, at one end.

4. Put the horn or other instrument in the opposite end of the basket and add greens and the rest of the music-related objects. If you have smaller instruments than those shown here, place them on little boxes hidden under the greens to raise them up.

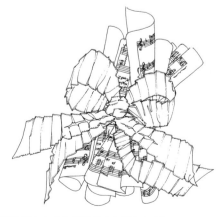

*U*se dried poinsettia "flowers" on wreaths, as tree ornaments, and in centerpieces to replace the all-too-common silk poinsettias that seem to appear everywhere. If you choose to hang this wreath, place it on an interior wall, rather than on your front door, to protect the fragile blooms.

Dried Poinsettia Wreath

The Color Theme

From deepest garnet to cream with splashes of pink, new poinsettia varieties are a testament to the plant breeder's art and science. When dried, the color of the bracts softens, so start with a vivid red or bright coral rather than one of the more pastel tones. If you are planning to hang this wreath rather than use it as a centerpiece, as shown on the opposite page, add a wire hanger before attaching the flowers because they are delicate when dried.

A Great Bargain

Immediately after Christmas, when gift wrap and cards go on half-price sale, garden centers are ready to toss poinsettia plants on the compost heap. While cards and decorations can be stored in basements until next year, live plants cannot. Buy floriferous plants at this time, at 80 percent (or more) off the regular price. Most garden centers are ready to make a deal on price. Dry the bracts and leaves and store them flat in a cardboard box with a lid in a dry place for use next holiday season.

Materials

Green sheet moss, 15 × 15 inches
11 dried poinsettia "flowers" (really bracts) in any color or mixed colors (See "Drying Poinsettias" on page 130 for instructions.)
8 to 10 small dried leaves
12 sprigs of honesty, 4 inches long, sprayed with gold paint
10 floral pins
14-inch-diameter polystyrene wreath form
Hot glue gun and glue sticks

---

1. Pin the sheet moss over the foam wreath to cover. Pull apart the sheet moss if necessary to make it fit.

2. Glue on the dried poinsettias and leaves.

3. Stick the sprigs of gold honesty into the wreath among the poinsettias.

Drying Poinsettias

To dry poinsettias, you will need:

Poinsettia plant

Pruning shears or scissors

3 cups of silica gel

8 × 8-inch plastic container with lid, or any size container that will hold one flower and fit in your microwave oven

Microwavable cup filled with water

Paper towels

Dust mask or respirator (I always use one when working with silica gel.)

Cut one "flower" from the plant with the shortest stem possible. The stem will exude a sticky sap. Wipe this end on a paper towel.

Pour half of the silica gel in the bottom of the plastic container. Nestle the flower on top. Carefully pour the rest of the silica gel around the edges. Then build up the sides and top so the flower is completely buried in silica gel.

Put the lid on the container but leave it slightly ajar. Put the cup of water in the back of the microwave and then put the container with the flower and silica gel in the microwave.

Turn the microwave on high power for 2 minutes, then let stand for 30 seconds before removing the container. Let cool for 10 minutes with the lid ajar to allow steam to escape.

Gently pour the silica gel back into its original container and place the "flower" on paper towels to complete its drying.

Repeat the process with each "flower." Once you get in the swing, it will take less time. The silica gel will still be slightly warm when you start the next flower. If the leaves are small, you can dry several at one time in a container. If you have more silica gel and another container, you can speed the process by drying a second flower while the first is cooling.

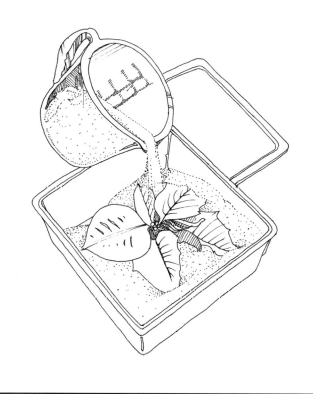

Check the inside of the microwave for moisture beads, and dry the surface with paper towels as needed.

The length of the poinsettia-drying process depends on the wattage of your microwave oven, the dryness of your silica gel, the size and moisture content of your flower, and probably some other factors I don't know about. Rather than be a slave to a recipe, you will have to adjust the timing as you go along.

If the "flower" doesn't seem quite dry enough, add another 15 seconds. If you are working with a small flower and warm silica gel, subtract 15 to 30 seconds. Remember, however, that the flowers will continue to firm up as they cool and continue to dry in the air. If the silica gel gets too damp, dry it in the oven as suggested in "Desiccant Drying" on page 39.

If you are not using the poinsettias immediately, store them flat in a cardboard box with a lid when they are completely dry.

*A*s the spiral turns gently in slow-wafting drafts,
clear lollipops and dried lemon slices filter the
light from the window and seem to activate the design.

Spiral Wreath

The Color Theme

When light pours through windows in churches, it enlivens the work of stained-glass artists. The effect of light through a window is the same as it shines through these homey decorations, giving them a warm glow. Choose any other Christmas ornaments that are enhanced by light and movement, like translucent glass balls, to show off the spiral wreath to best effect.

Materials

9 strands of pliable grapevine, 14 feet long
Coil of 9-gauge wire
Heavy-duty wire cutters
Brown floral wrapping tape
24-gauge floral spool wire
26 assorted translucent, colored lollipops
19 dried lemon slices
32 sprigs of pine or other evergreens, 4 to 6 inches long
Hot glue gun and glue sticks

1. Stretch out the grapevine on the ground in one pile.

2. Cut off about 14 feet of 9-gauge wire from the coil and wrap brown tape all along this wire. Do not stretch out the wire, but wrap it still coiled.

3. This is the only hard part of the project. If you can borrow an extra pair of hands at this point, please do so. Take the spool wire and

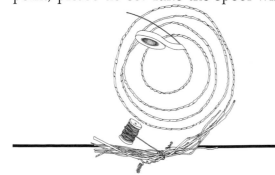

wrap the grapevine to the 9-gauge wire. The wire will be practically invisible when you are finished. Trim off any uneven ends from top or bottom.

4. Now, coil this wired vine as tightly as you can to make a flat wreath. The more compactly you do this, the nicer your finished spiral will be. This wreath has five coils and stretches to about 3 feet long.

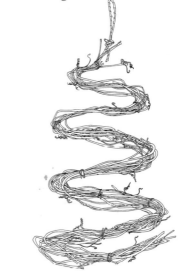

5. Place something heavy such as books or bricks on the flat coil for three to five days to help it rest in this position.

6. When you are ready to hang and decorate the spiral, cut off a 6-inch piece of the spool wire and attach it to the top of the spiral and make a loop. Hang the spiral in your designated spot and decorate right there after the spiral has uncoiled.

7. Decorate the spiral by tucking the lollipop sticks right through the vines. Tuck or glue other decorations such as lemon slices and evergreen sprigs to the grapevine. After Christmas, remove the decorations, recoil the spiral, and store it for next year.

*U*se these baskets as accent pieces, as containers for other decorations, or as gifts. The fabric basket involves no sewing and can be constructed in different sizes, shapes, and patterns. Take any of these trim ideas and spruce up your basket collection for the holidays.

A Trio of Christmas Baskets

The Color Theme

I chose traditional Christmas greens and reds for the decorations but varied the tones of each color. Colors of natural materials usually blend well and here the reds are all deep shades, from the cranberries in glass to the wine color of the dried sumac decorating the fabric basket. The greens range from the soft yellow-green of the sheet moss in the wire basket to the bright green of the boxwood trim on the fabric basket.

Wire Basket with Galax "Rose" Materials

Fresh or dried sheet moss, 12 × 12 inches
6 fresh galax leaves
7 catalpa pods or other large pods like locust
Materials for inside decoration, such as pinecones, magnolia cones with red seeds, additional catalpa pods, and fresh or dried red fruit from Kousa dogwood
Any nice basket (Here I used a galvanized wire basket in an old French design.)
2 feet of 22- to 26-gauge floral spool wire
Green floral wrapping tape
Pruning shears or scissors

1. If the moss is dried, dampen it with water. This will prevent crumbling and refresh the green color. Spread the moss over the bottom and sides of the basket, faceup.

2. To make the galax "rose," cut the stems off the leaves. Take the smallest leaf and roll it into a tube, letting the top flare out slightly. Pinch the bottom together. Continue to hold the pinch.

3. Take the next-smallest leaf and wrap that around the first tube, like the petal of a flower, and pinch at the bottom.

About Galax Leaves

Galax leaves are inexpensive to buy at your local florist, and they last up to three weeks in a fresh arrangement. The galax "rose" pictured here was made of fresh leaves. The rose will dry in place and make a lovely green ornament.

4. Continue wrapping each leaf around the cluster in your hand, each time centering the new leaf around the opening of the cluster. While I have used six leaves here, you can add additional leaves if you wish to make a bigger rose.

5. Wrap the spool wire tightly around the base of the rose cluster to secure the bundle of leaves. Cover the wire with green floral wrapping tape, then tie the rose to the handle of the basket with the wire.

6. Tie catalpa pods to the handle with wire.

7. Tuck a small piece of sheet moss over the wire to hide it from view.

8. Arrange the pinecones, magnolia cones, and other decorative materials inside the basket by simply laying them on the moss.

(continued on next page)

Glass Basket with Bear Grass Bow Materials

One or two bags of fresh cranberries
12 to 15 strands of fresh bear grass
Sprig of holly with berries
Stems of fresh greens like pine (optional)
Glass basket
Pruning shears or scissors
12 inches of thin-gauge floral spool wire, such as 24 or 26
Hot glue gun and glue sticks, or thick white craft glue

1. Wash and pick over the cranberries. Discard any soft or rotten ones. Pour the others into the glass basket, then fill the basket with water. (Note: If you put the water in first, the berries will all float and you will have a difficult time, so follow the suggested order.)

2. To make the bow, clip off about 3 inches from the white end (bottom) of the bear grass and discard. Grasp the stems all together in the middle. Make a loop on one side, then on the other. Bind the loops in the center with the wire. Use the remainder of the wire to attach the bow to the base of the basket handle.

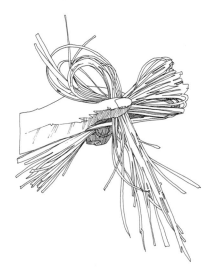

3. Glue a sprig of holly to the bow to cover the wiring mechanics.

4. Add stems of fresh greens like pine to the cranberries and water to make a small informal arrangement, if desired. The cranberries will hold the stems in place and add color to a simple design. They will remain fresh for three to four weeks if you add fresh water.

Fabric Basket Materials

4 small clusters of sumac or other dried berries
4 sprigs of boxwood or other greens
Old newspaper
1 cup fabric stiffener
½ cup water
Large bowl
12 × 24-inch piece of fabric in Christmas colors
Spoon
Waxed paper or waxed freezer paper
Plastic pint freezer food container
Scissors
Ruler
4 large safety pins
Hot glue gun and glue sticks, or thick white craft glue

1. Spread your work surface with newspapers to catch the drips. Mix the fabric stiffener and water in the large bowl.

2. Immerse the fabric in the mixture and stir around with the spoon, until the fabric is completely coated. Lay a 3-foot piece of waxed paper on your covered work surface.

3. Remove the fabric and let it drain over the bowl. With your hands (you can't help getting messy) press out excess stiffener from the fabric. Don't wring it out; try to prevent wrinkling the fabric more than necessary.

4. Lay the fabric pattern-side-down on the waxed paper. Turn up a ½-inch hem around all four sides and press the hem flat with your finger.

5. Now fold the fabric in half to make a square. Press all the edges together. You will now have a fabric square about 11 × 11 inches with smooth edges and pattern on both sides.

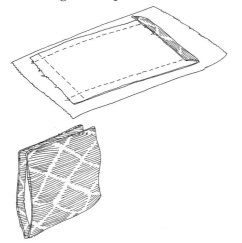

6. Turn the pint container upside down. Drape the fabric square over this mold and center it as evenly as possible. Let the four corners flare outward and pin each corner together with a safety pin.

7. Let the fabric dry. It will take one to two days. To remove the formed basket from the mold, slightly squeeze the plastic and the sides will release.

> **Diversify**
>
> To make baskets in other shapes and sizes, look for different "molds." A woman's shoe box is a good size for a low, rectangular basket. Drape any cardboard mold with waxed paper before covering with fabric for easy removal of the finished basket. Measure all around the mold to get the size fabric that you need. Don't forget to add an allowance for the hems, then double the total measurement.

8. Remove the safety pins. The interior of the basket may still be damp, but the shape will hold. Let it finish drying before decorating.

9. To decorate, glue small clusters of leaves and berries in the four corners, facing outward.

*T*he African American holiday Kwanzaa is a harvest celebration. Starting December 26 and for seven days thereafter, families light a candle and discuss one of seven principles of daily living, including collective work and responsibility, creativity, and faith.

Kwanzaa Celebration

The Color Theme

The concept of Kwanzaa was created in 1965 by Maulana Karenga, Ph.D., a Black studies professor who wanted to emphasize elements of Pan-African heritage and pride for black Americans. The colors of the candles—black, red, and green—are the colors of the flag of the African National Congress. They have come to symbolize Africa for many.

Each child in the family is represented by an ear of corn on the celebratory table. Other colors abound as fruits of the harvest are displayed. African crafts like this Kente cloth from Ghana add to the theme of heritage. Other symbols, traditions, and foods are described in the book *Kwanzaa: An African American Celebration of Culture and Cooking*.

Materials

16 pieces of dried stalk like broom corn, sorghum, or bamboo, 9 inches long

16 pieces of dried stalk, 4 inches long

Assorted dried leaves, pods, and grains (Here I've used wheat, sea oats, yarrow, Japanese lantern pods picked before turning orange, smooth sumac, and eucalyptus leaves and berries.)

4 × 3 × 9-inch block of brown floral foam

Ruler

Serrated bread knife or other sharp knife

6 candle prongs

1 taller candle prong

Hot glue gun and glue sticks

Pruning shears or scissors

Flame retardant spray (available at hardware stores)

7 tapered candles in black, red, and green (Here I've used 1 black and 3 each of green and red.)

1. Put the foam on the table. Mark ½ inch in from the edge on the long side.

2. With the knife, slice the block of foam on a slant toward the bottom, making a pyramid. The base will remain 4 inches wide for stability, but the top will be narrower.

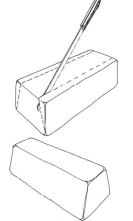

3. The seven candle prongs will fit edge to edge in a row along the top of the pyramid. Start at one end and push the prong snugly into the foam. Insert the next one abutting, and so on down the row. Put the one taller prong in the middle.

4. Glue eight long pieces of stalk to the foam on the long side, starting at the bottom. Fit each piece snugly against the previous one to hide the foam. Repeat on the other long side.

5. Now cover the short sides with the short pieces of stalk. Because of the pyramid shape, after the bottom piece is glued on, the next pieces will have to be trimmed slightly with the pruning shears as you go.

6. Glue leaves, pods, and grains to the top of the candleholder, but keep plant materials well away from the candle bottoms.

7. Spray the completed project with flame retardant, then insert the seven candles. When you use this project or any other with candles, never leave a lit candle unattended.

*T*his romantic heart of dried lavender and roses
emits subtle whiffs of fragrance on tiny currents of
air. For more intense fragrance, sprinkle a drop or two of
essential oil of rose or lavender on the foliage.

Valentine Heart

The Color Theme

For Saint Valentine's Day, reds and pinks predominate and, of all flowers, the rose is most popular. Fresh roses last but a brief moment; dried roses look lovely for years. If you receive a bouquet of fresh roses, set them to dry within a few days to preserve the best color. Don't think you can wait until they are practically dead and then have perfect dried roses.

Materials

One bunch of fresh Scotch broom stems, not in flower (about 6 stems, 2 feet tall)
3 dried red roses
7 dried pink or peach roses
Dried lavender
1 yard of 16-gauge wire
Green floral wrapping tape
Pruning shears or scissors
22- or 24-gauge floral spool wire
1 strand of pink raffia or narrow pink ribbon

1. Form the 16-gauge wire into a loop and twine the two ends around each other to secure.

2. Wrap the loop with the floral wrapping tape, pulling gently as you wrap, and overlapping as you go.

3. To make the heart shape, indent the top of the loop about 3 inches.

4. Cut the Scotch broom into 6- to 7-inch-

long pieces. Sometimes you will have a whole cluster on one stem and sometimes you will have to remove the "needles" from the stem and form your own cluster. Cut off ungainly thick stems that show from the top of a cluster.

5. Tie the end of the spool wire to the bottom of the heart wreath form.

6. Take a small cluster of Scotch broom and bind it to the wreath form with the spool wire, with stems pointing upward. Bind on additional clusters all around the form, putting each new cluster over the stems of the one before. Make the clusters very narrow where the heart dips down at the top and bind them closely to the form.

7. For the decoration, make a separate bouquet of roses and lavender and tie with the raffia or ribbon, making a bow. The bouquet should be about 9 inches tall.

8. Attach the bouquet to the heart wreath in two places with spool wire by first taking a 6-inch length of wire and tying the bouquet to the indent of the heart. Then take a 12-inch piece of wire and tie it at the base of the bouquet near the raffia bow. Bring the ends up behind the bouquet and attach to the top of the heart.

9. Hang it from a hook, or place it against your lover's pillow to whisper a secret message.

*T*he dreary winter has ended and spring blossoms forth, signaling new beginnings. The egg, symbolizing spring in many cultures, is roasted for the Passover plate and decorated, hunted, and dyed for Easter. Here the shell serves as a perfect watertight container for the small flowers that announce the glorious springtime unfolding of the earth.

Spring Vases

The Color Theme

Do you have fond memories of dying Easter eggs at home, at school, or at Scouts? Did those dye pills ever dissolve? If you enjoyed the garish colors of the packaged dyes then, you may want more subtlety now. While these shell vases are beautiful in their natural shades of white or brown, try one the natural plant dyes on page 21 for the Easter season. My favorite is beet juice for an easy, gentle pink (and you can make a salad with the cold beets).

Egg-Citing Variations

If available, use goose, duck, or turkey eggs for larger vases. Black metal apple stackers can often hold larger eggshells, especially if lined around the rims with moss. You can sometimes make vases from the empty eggshells of songbirds, too. Use robins' eggs nesting in green moss for minuscule arrangements.

Instead of using an egg holder, as shown in the photo on the opposite page, group several egg cups for your arrangement, and put a shell vase and flowers in each. Scatter any extra shells on the table to complete the decoration.

Materials

1 to 3 stems of fresh flowers for each egg vase
6 to 12 jumbo-size eggs, brown or white
Pointed paring knife
Clean bowl
Soap and water
Natural dyes like beet juice (see page 21) or other vegetable dyes (optional)
Metal egg stand

1. Crack each egg at the pointed end with the paring knife. Remove a small amount of shell. Pour the egg into the clean bowl to save for cooking. You may have to use the knife to mix up the egg in the shell in order to get the egg to slip out. Refrigerate the "scrambled" eggs for later use in omelets, fritattas, popovers, pancakes, or whatever.

2. Wash the shells carefully in soapy water to remove all traces of egg. Dye the shells as desired.

3. The shell vases will have jagged edges and be uneven in size. That is part of their charm. Place them carefully in the egg stand and add water. Arrange small bunches of spring flowers and leaves in each. Keep the flower and foliage stems short so they will fit in. Here I've used lentin rose, an early-blooming, shade-loving perennial.

*D*ried flowers are as appropriate in spring as fresh ones if the colors are vibrant and in keeping with the holiday theme. Make this Easter centerpiece well ahead of a family brunch and have one less last-minute concern.

The oval shape of the arrangement follows the tradition of egg decoration, symbolizing rebirth and regeneration in springtime.

Easter Egg Centerpiece

The Color Theme

My early spring garden is replete with gold and purple crocus, glowing forsythia, daffodils, and grape hyacinth. I plant pansies each year by April 1 and their blooms cheer me—yellow and blue of course, but also some of the newer peaches and pinks. Although the timing of Easter varies, the garden always offers something for a fresh arrangement.

In this dried centerpiece, the challenge is to make the arrangement as springlike as fresh-picked flowers. Purple and yellow are traditional for Easter, and here I've included as many shades of each as I had available. Pastels, such as pink and peach, light blue, and green would also be appropriate for spring.

Materials

Green sheet moss, approximately 18 × 25 inches
Dried flowers in yellows, golds, purples, and lavenders (Here I've used 17 roses, 39 strawflowers, 8 stems of purple statice, 8 stems of lavender statice, 8 stems of purple larkspur, and 18 globe thistles.)
Paring knife
3 bricks of green floral foam
Oval tray, platter, or flat basket (Here I've used a 12 × 17-inch platter.)
6 inches of floral clay
6 floral prongs
6 to 8 floral pins
Pruning shears or scissors
Hot glue gun and glue sticks

1. With the paring knife, trim the bricks of floral foam to fit the bottom of the oval container. Remove the foam and set aside.

2. Put 1 inch of floral clay at the bottom of each floral prong and press the prongs firmly to the bottom of the container.

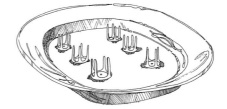

3. Replace the foam in the container, setting it on top of the prongs, which will hold it in place.

4. Use the paring knife again to trim away the angles, making a rounded oval of the foam. Work slowly, shaving off some here and there. When you are satisfied, cover all the foam with sheet moss and pin it in place with the floral pins.

5. Now put the flowers in rows across the oval. I started with a center row of roses, but slanted the row across the bias rather than running it straight up the center. Cut the stems of the roses about 2 inches long with a point at the end. The point helps to pierce the moss and foam. Start inserting roses at one edge and work up and over the top to the other edge. Then do the next row in your choice of flowers and continue until the oval is covered. Flowers such as the larkspur should be cut in 2-inch lengths and glued to the moss on their sides.

Make a wreath with dried garlic to scare away the vampires, a lurking spider to scare away the humans, and bleached "devil's-claws" to scare away the animals. Wrap in a giant web of intrigue.

Scared Silly

The Color Theme

White ghosts, black cats and witches, orange pumpkins—the colors of Halloween are immutable. In this wreath, the orange Japanese lantern pods are accents to the theme of ghostly white. Baby Boo miniature pumpkins and other white gourds, garlic, and bleached pods dominate the decoration. The black spider (widow or widower) is waiting to pounce on its next victim.

Materials

6 pieces of vine, 3 to 4 feet long
Assortment of 10 miniature white pumpkins and gourds
6 fresh or dried garlic heads
8 bleached devil's-claws (martynia pods; see page 22 for instructions on bleaching pods)
20 Japanese lantern pods
21 pressed golden fall leaves
Hot glue gun and glue sticks
12 floral picks, 6 inches long
Ice pick or sharp skewer
Pruning shears or scissors
Pack of spider webbing (available in season at variety stores)
Purchased artificial spider

1. To make the wreath, grasp a piece of vine in one hand, 10 inches from the thick end.

2. With your other hand, form the vine into a circle, about 18 inches in diameter. Keep wrapping in and out around the circle until that piece of vine is used up. Tuck in the end.

3. Take the next piece of vine and repeat Step 2, allowing 8 to 10 inches of vine to point outward, then wrap the rest of the vine in and out around the circle. Continue with all the other pieces of vine. This wreath should require no wiring because the strands of vine wrap around each other and hold themselves.

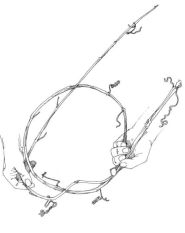

4. To decorate, group the decorations in three major clusters. Start with the pumpkins and the gourds. Hot-glue one or two in each cluster directly to the wreath. If they don't fit into the vine easily, you'll need to use the floral picks.

5. Poke a small hole in the bottom of the remaining gourds and pumpkins with the ice pick or skewer. Insert a floral pick in the hole until it is secure. The wooden pick will slowly swell with moisture from the fruit, keeping it in place. (See "Treating Fruits for Longer Life" on page 149 for suggestions on making gourds last.) Insert the other end of the pick between the vines of the wreath and glue in place. If the pick is too long, cut off the exposed end with the pruning shears.

6. Glue on the garlic and the devil's-claw in each cluster.

7. Glue the Japanese lantern pods and pressed fall leaves among the clusters and in other bare spots.

8. Glue the spider to the twigs that stick out.

9. Take the purchased webbing and stretch some out over the whole wreath. Tuck the ends in the back of the wreath; it will hold by itself. I only used about one-fifth of a small pack for this wreath. The more you stretch it, the more natural it looks.

A traditional cornucopia sings of the fall harvest. It welcomes family and guests to your home in a way few other arrangements do. Here it fills the entrance of an unused bake oven in my kitchen fireplace.

Giving Thanks

The Color Theme

Fruits and vegetables in red, orange, and yellow and grains in honey beige and brown—these are fall harvest colors in the East. Blue and bright green seem out of place in Thanksgiving decorations because we take the colors from the materials at hand in November.

I've used a mixture of fruits and grains from my own garden, produce from local stands, and "weeds" from the roadside to achieve a bountiful look. Gather more material than you think you will need as it is important that this arrangement look lush and overflowing.

Materials

Mixture of dried grains, grasses, fresh fruits, gourds, and berries (Here I've used Indian finger corn, strawberry corn, foxtail millet, black-bearded wheat, sea oats, setaria, miniature pumpkins, rose hips, fresh hot peppers, and crab apples from the flowering crab tree.)

2 pieces of fresh vine, 2 to 3 feet long, stripped of leaves

Cornucopia basket or other basket

8 to 10 floral picks, 6 inches long

Treating Fruits for Longer Life

Allow decorative corn to air-dry in your home, spread out on a rack. Make sure the leaves are dry or they will mildew in your arrangement.

If you grow your own pumpkins and gourds, let them mature on the vine until the stems turn brown. Cut with the stem intact.

Wash gourds, pumpkins, and crab apples in water and detergent to remove all dirt. Then soak in a solution of 1 part liquid bleach to 2 parts water for about 20 minutes to kill surface bacteria that speed rotting.

Pour acrylic floor wax into an old coffee can or pan. Dip the crab apples, gourds, and pumpkins in the wax, remove, shake, and let drain and dry on a brown paper bag. The floor wax can be poured back into the bottle, kept, and reused from year to year.

Some miniature pumpkins will last for six months or more treated in this way. Others won't, even following all the proper instructions. They have a mind of their own.

---

1. Clean and prepare the fruit according to directions in "Treating Fruits for Longer Life" on the right.

2. Stuff the inside end of the cornucopia basket with small fruits to the tip. Keep building up and out with slightly larger materials. Add stems of grains in small bunches to help wedge the materials in place.

3. Let the material tumble out of the mouth of the basket. Where the stems are not long enough, push a floral pick into the bottom of the fruit or vegetable. Insert that stem into the body of the arrangement. Hide the pick if it shows by placing other grains on top.

4. If using a basket with a square or rectangular bottom, turn it on its side and make your arrangement in the same way as in the cornucopia. Wire or glue some of the material to the basket's top surface to help disguise the shape.

5. For the final placement of materials, put the cornucopia in its proper place and finish your construction there.

6. Wrap each piece of vine around the whole construction and tuck in the ends to secure them.

Making a Bow

It's often best to attach a bow to a dried flower project near the beginning of construction so as not to disturb the fragile flowers once they are in place. Here's the basic bow-making technique that I use. For an easy and attractive bow, use ribbon that is wired down both sides.

Materials

2 yards of ribbon
6 inches of thin wire
Scissors

1. Place the ribbon flat in your palm and hold it under your thumb 11 inches from one end.

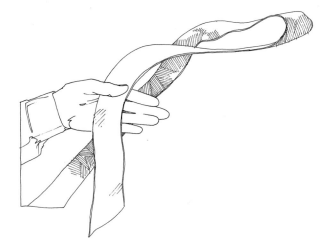

2. With the longer "tail" of ribbon, make a loop 4 inches long and hold it under your thumb.

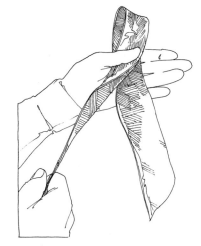

3. Make another 4-inch loop in the opposite direction and secure it with your thumb.

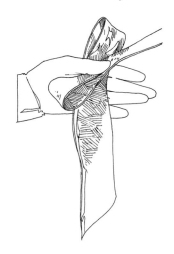

4. Continue forming additional pairs of loops to the left and right, each time making the pairs about ½ inch smaller. You will have enough ribbon to make two to four pairs of loops.

5. Still holding the bow under your thumb, make one small loop of ribbon in the center, about 1 inch in diameter. Let the tail come down behind this small loop.

6. Put the wire through the center of the small loop and pull tightly behind the bow. Twist the wire to secure all the loops.

7. Cut the tails of the ribbon on an angle, and perk up the loops of the bow as desired.

8. Use the extra wire to attach the bow to your project.

Glossary of Craft Materials

The craft materials listed here are available in craft shops, from florists, in floral supply departments, and in some hardware stores.

Alum: A preservative used as a mordant in dyes. It's available in the spice section of your supermarket or by mail order. (See "Sources" on page 154.)

Candle prong: Made of plastic; one end is pointed to insert into floral foam, fruit, or vegetables; the other end supports the candle.

Fabric stiffener: Use Aleene's or another brand; follow package directions.

Flame retardant: Spray arranged flowers that will be used around candles to help them resist burning; follow package directions. Never leave treated or untreated plant materials unattended around open flames.

Floral clay: Comes in a roll protected with paper on one side; has the consistency of chewing gum. To use, tear off about 1 inch, remove the paper, and stretch out the clay. Then press the clay on the article you wish to adhere. Make sure the article is completely dry, or the clay won't stick. Floral clay works well on glass, plastic, polystyrene, and baskets.

Floral foam: For fresh flowers use green bricks, which absorb water. Before using, soak bricks in a bucket of water for 20 to 30 minutes until saturated. Never reuse green foam that has held fresh flowers; it could harbor destructive bacteria. Save unused chunks of foam that were cut off when shaping it. Use chunk foam in vases to hold stems in place. Or buy already shredded foam. For dry flowers use brown bricks, which are non-absorbent. Brown bricks specifically for dried material come in a hard foam, like polystyrene; use for thick stems and branches. Use softer brown foam for thin, delicate stems. To cut foam, use a sharp paring or steak knife.

Floral pick: Use to attach plant material to a wreath or to lengthen and strengthen stems of dried material in a flower arrangement. Different lengths are available. My favorite is a 4-inch pick with 6-inch wire attached. You can shorten the pick, if necessary, and cut a new point with pruning shears. To use, take a small bunch of stems and lay the bottom 2 inches of stems along the top 2 inches of the pick. Wrap the wire around the stems, then secure with a layer of floral wrapping tape. Remove the wire before inserting a pick into a fruit or vegetable.

Floral pin: Also called a greening pin. Essential for attaching material to a straw wreath base. The most versatile are the 1¾-inch pins.

Floral preservative or food for fresh flowers: Prevents bacterial growth. Use a powdered commercial product like Floral Life, or mix 3 drops of liquid bleach per pint of water.

Floral prong: Use to secure wet or dry foam to a container. Put a layer of floral clay on the bottom of the prong and press it down into the container. Place floral foam over the prong to secure it in place.

Floral wrapping tape: Comes in brown, green, white, and other colors. To use, gently pull out a length of tape to stretch it. Wrap a stem by overlapping the tape as you twist it around the stem. This tape sticks to itself but not to the stem or other things.

Glass marbles: Use clear or colored glass marbles at the bottom of a glass vase to hold stems in place. The heavier the stems, the more marbles you'll need to support them.

Glue, thick white craft: Use for pressed-flower work and many crafts in place of hot glue. It doesn't harden instantly as does hot glue; wait for it to set before continuing with your project.

Glue gun: Use a hot glue gun for all types of craft work unless directions specify otherwise. (Hot glue does not work well on metal.) Get a glue gun with self-advancing glue stick. Buy glue sticks that dry clear. Follow package directions. Keep fingers away from dribbling glue. Keep cold water handy for immediately dunking hot fingers into to reduce stinging and prevent blisters.

Cool glue guns are similar, but operate at cooler temperatures. The glue will not burn your fingers. Use for crafts that will be placed outdoors in hot sun or in below-freezing locations.

Knife, kitchen: A sharp kitchen knife is handy for trimming or cutting holes in fruits and vegetables. A paring or steak knife is good for cutting floral foam.

Knife, utility: Utility knives, like X-acto knives, are useful when working with pressed flowers or paper projects.

Pinholder: Also called a frog. Composed of sharp metal pins; ideal for small arrangements. Secure the pinholder to a base with floral clay.

Polystyrene: Available in many shapes, including bricks and spheres. Spheres are good for topiaries. Polystyrene is too hard to stick most flower stems into without breaking them; instead, attach your materials with glue or pins.

Raffia: A material from the Madagascar palm, used for making bows and knots. It comes dyed in different colors as well as natural. Strands are about 3 feet long.

Ribbon, paper: Comes in rolls, either twisted or untwisted. Buy by the yard or roll. To aid in untwisting, soak the ribbon in water for 5 minutes. Wring out excess water, gently untwist ribbon, and hang over a shower rod to dry. You can also use it straight from the roll as a colored cord in projects.

Scissors, household: Useful for cutting ribbon, paper, and thin or soft stems.

Shears, pruning: Useful for cutting thick or woody stems; wide variety available.

Silica gel: An excellent desiccant for drying special flowers. Has the appearance and consistency of white sugar. Always use a dust mask when working with it to prevent breathing the powder.

Spray, protective: True everlastings such as strawflowers need no protective spray. For more delicate flowers and those dried in silica gel, use spray lacquer, hair spray, or a special floral product like Super Surface Sealer spray. Spray a light coat over both the front and back of the flower; add a second coat once the first coat is dry. Several light coats are better than one thick layer.

Spray adhesive: Helpful when you're working with Spanish moss. A light coat of spray will help the moss hold together and give it a smoother look.

Wire, floral (stub): Comes precut in different gauges (widths). Higher-number gauges indicate thinner wire. Buy 16- or 18-gauge for thicker wire, 22 or 24 for thinner wire. "Bright" stub wire looks silvery when new, darkens over time, and rusts when wet; ideal to use for wiring strawflowers and globe amaranths.

Wire, floral spool: Green-coated; comes in different gauges (widths). Higher-number gauges indicate thinner wire. Use 22- or 24-gauge for wrapping material to wreath frames or topiary forms.

Wire cutters: Handy for trimming all kinds of floral wire.

Wreath frame: Inexpensive and comes readymade in different designs and sizes for different purposes. Use a flat wire frame when wrapping dried material to the frame with floral spool wire. Try a box wire frame when wrapping fresh greens to the frame with floral spool wire. Use floral pins to attach fresh or dried plant materials to a straw wreath base. Hillman wreath forms come in a variety of shapes and sizes with clasps permanently attached to the forms; you need nothing else for attaching fresh or dried materials.

Sources

The Cook's Garden
P.O. Box 76
Londonberry, VT 05148
(802) 824-5526
A good source for sunflowers.

Dorothy Biddle Service
Box 900
Greeley, PA 18425
(717) 226-3239
Floral arranging supplies and retail catalog.

J & T Imports
143 S. Cedros Ave.
Solana Beach, CA 92075
(619) 481-9781
Large variety of high-quality dried flowers.

Johnny's Selected Seeds
2580 Foss Hill Rd.
Albion, ME 04910
(207) 437-9294
Large variety of garden seeds excellent for cooler areas.

The Mannings
Box 687
East Berlin, PA 17316
(800) 223-7166
Source for alum and other dyeing and weaving supplies.

Meadow Lark Flower & Herb Farm
R.D. 1 Box 1568
Orwigsburg, PA 17961
(717) 366-1618
No catalog available.

Park Seed Co.
P.O. Box 31
Cokesbury Rd.
Greenwood, SC 29647
(803) 223-7333
Good prices on many varieties of dried flowers.

Thompson & Morgan, Inc.
P.O. Box 1308
Jackson, NJ 08527
(908) 363-2225
Huge variety of seeds, flowers, and grasses for drying.

Suggested Reading

Here are some books you may want to peruse for floral craft ideas and information.

Copage, Eric V. *Kwanzaa: An African American Celebration of Culture and Cooking*. New York: Morrow, 1991. *Describes important symbols, traditions, and foods of the Kwanzaa celebration.*

Grae, Ida. *Nature's Colors*. New York: Macmillan, 1974. *A good resource for dyeing with plant materials.*

Kowalchik, Claire, and William H. Hylton, eds. *Rodale's Illustrated Encyclopedia of Herbs*. Emmaus, Pa.: Rodale Press, 1987. *A compendium of information on culinary and ornamental herbs and their uses, including information on dyeing with herbs.*

Platt, Ellen Spector. *Flower Crafts*. Emmaus, Pa.: Rodale Press, 1993. *More information on growing flowers for drying. Over 50 flower craft designs with complete instructions, color photos, and illustrations.*

Robertson, Seonaid. *Dyes from Plants*. New York: Van Nostrand Reinhold Co., 1973. *More information on dyeing with plant materials.*

Index

Note: Page references in *italic* indicate tables. **Boldface** references indicate photographs.